The Politics of
Writing
Centers

CHARLES I. SCHUSTER, SERIES EDITOR

The Politics of
Writing
Centers

Edited by

Jane Nelson and Kathy Evertz

Foreword by John Trimbur

Boynton/Cook Publishers
HEINEMANN
Portsmouth, NH

Boynton/Cook Publishers, Inc.
A subsidiary of Reed Elsevier Inc.
361 Hanover Street
Portsmouth, NH 03801–3912
www.boyntoncook.com

Offices and agents throughout the world

Library of Congress Cataloging-in-Publication Data
The politics of writing centers / edited by Jane Nelson and Kathy Evertz ; foreword by John Trimbur.
     p. cm. — (CrossCurrents)
     Includes bibliographical references.
     ISBN 0-86709-569-5 (pbk. : acid-free paper)
     1. English language—Rhetoric—Study and teaching. 2. Report writing—Study and teaching (Higher). 3. Interdisciplinary approach in education. 4. Writing centers—Political aspects. I. Nelson, Jane V. II. Evertz, Kathy. III. CrossCurrents (Portsmouth, N.H.).

PE1404 .P577 2001
808'.042'0711—dc21   2001025418

Consulting editor: Charles I. Schuster
Editor: Lisa Luedeke
Production: Vicki Kasabian
Cover design: Tom Allen
Manufacturing: Steve Bernier

Printed in the United States of America on acid-free paper
05 04 03 02 01 DA 1 2 3 4 5

Contents

Part 2: The Politics of Location

Foreword

The collection of essays you're holding has caused me—and, I think, will cause anyone who has been involved, directly or indirectly, in writing-center work—to reflect on what the editors Jane Nelson and Kathy Evertz properly call "the terrain of power in which writing centers are located." As you will see, Nelson and Evertz chart this terrain in terms of the overlapping politics of conversation (how writing centers represent their work to themselves and to others, and how they think about tutorial talk) and of location (how writing centers are articulated to institutional settings). This volume, however, doesn't just summarize what is already known about the politics of writing centers; it looks closely (through a collective effort) at writing-center work, to note critical absences, and to see anew—or, as the editors say, "to be on the lookout for what one isn't thinking."

This emphasis on the not-quite-imagined at the edge of thought is, for me, the key to this collection. By this point, there has been a considerable (and helpful) critical body of work on writing centers. Certainly writing centers know much more about theory and practice than was true, say, when I got started directing writing centers in the 1970s. Over the past thirty years, writing-center inquiry has turned from anecdotal exchanges and program descriptions into a systematic exploration of the meanings and potentialities of writing centers. We have more intellectual and practical means at our disposal these days to think about writing centers. The contributors acknowledge the importance of this work—and then seek to push it forward, straining against the edges of the "best available practice."

"Pushing forward," of course, is no easy matter, and I'm not about to pretend there's an inexorable logic that moves writing centers in ever more progressive and sophisticated directions. Instead, it's better to think of writing-center work as what the sociologist of science Andrew Pickering calls the "mangle of practice"—that partly theorized, partly improvised activity of experimentation that scientists use to deal with the recalcitrant realities of the natural world. Analogously, writing-center directors are caught up in a dialectic of resistance and accommodation, where they try to cope, as best they might, with the pressures and limits of life in academic institutions. Let me give you three examples of writing centers I've been involved with to get a sense of how the "mangle of practice" plays out in particular settings.

In an open-admissions community college in the 1970s, this institution had just shifted from the old junior-college model of providing two years of lower-division work for students preparing to transfer to four-year colleges. Virtually overnight, the student body changed from predominantly white, Euro-American, college-bound, eighteen- to twenty-two-year-olds to older returning students, predominantly African American and largely inner-city single women looking for vocational training to get off welfare and out of the reserve army of labor. In a response typical of the time, the English faculty devised a three-tiered writing sequence—a course each on the sentence, paragraph, and essay—driven by drills and skills. The writing center was seen as a cost-effective supplement to reinforce classroom instruction by review and practice.

Consequently, the tutor training sessions I led were in many ways the most politically charged of any I've ever experienced. In fact, to call them "training" doesn't really capture the feel of those meetings at all. They were agonized political discussions about our responsibilities to students, the writing faculty, and the institution. If anything, the difficulties only intensified as the tutors began to recognize that the college's open door was too often a revolving one and that the writing curriculum was disciplining and sorting students but not teaching very many of them to write. The tutors' response, which I endorsed, was to "teach the test" in the double sense of term: to help as many students as possible to succeed on the endless grammar quizzes (and thus to acquire needed credentials) and, at the same time, to explain how testing itself works in the culture of schooling so that the students who failed would not internalize failure as a personal defeat.

In a state college in the 1980s, this college enrolled mostly white "ethnics," first-generation working-class and lower middle-class students looking for upper mobility in human services, teaching, management, and the new information economies. Influenced by the process movement and New Leftist, countercultural suspicions of all forms of traditional authority, the writing center sought, with remarkable success, to build a community of writers in a semiautonomous space outside the classroom and the official curriculum.

There was, of course, a good deal of tutoring the usual writing assignments. But what really marked this center in my mind was the amount of extracurricular writing that took place by tutors and tutees alike. I don't think I'm romanticizing the moment to say the tutors, according to Stephen North's famous maxim, were working to "produce better writers not better writings"—to rehabilitate, as it were, the writer from the pupil. There was a deeply felt sense that students had been damaged by schooling, that classroom life was inhospitable, and that new forums for writing were not only needed but possible.

In a technological university in the 1990s, the small engineering school, like the state college I just described, has traditionally been a means of upward mobility, though in this case for the technically inclined sons and daughters of southern New England's ethnic class cultures. Defining features, at least for the writing center, are the university's project-based learning, its emphasis on teamwork, and the absence of a first-year writing requirement. Faculty are seen as mentors instead of adversaries, and, accordingly, the writing center provides "dedicated" tutors for individual courses and projects (a practice about which I had once held serious reservations) to support writing across the curriculum. The approach is less ideological, more eclectic, and more rhetorical. We are currently transforming the writing center into a multiliteracy center that offers tutoring in oral presentations and visual design, as well as writing. Like so many other writing centers, we are trying to figure out what it might mean to be online.

I offer these accounts of three writing centers in part as emblematic trends in the shared histories of writing-center work. These accounts—and all the others like them in the writing-center archive—can help characterize the politics of writing centers in their simplest and perhaps most profound sense, as a matter of how people organize themselves to work with other people on shared projects at a particular time and place. Politics, in such accounts, involves the identifications and divisions entailed in trying to accomplish such work.

But there is also another, nagging term in these accounts, which I'll call "outcomes." What I mean is not the outcomes used to measure in assessing a writing center's work with tutees. Instead, I mean the larger political outcomes about the organization and consolidation of cultural capital. To see how this works, I want to close by describing what happened to the tutors who worked in the centers I've described.

- Of the best tutors in the 1970s open-admissions community college writing center, one died young of a heart attack, another got a scholarship to a liberal arts college, a third (a gifted musician) was playing the blues in small clubs, and the fourth wrote bad checks and, the last I heard, was on the lam with her drug-dealing boyfriend.

- The tutors at the 1980s state college have gone into adult literacy work and received Ph.D.s (and now tenure) in rhetoric and composition. Others are teaching in high schools, writing for local newspapers, and working in public relations, publishing, and technical writing.

- The tutors at the 1990s technological university are now employed (and moving up) in high-tech firms or pursuing graduate education—cashing in, justly enough from the perspective of their individual talents and efforts, on the scandalous inequities of a "new prosperity" brought about by the globalization of finance capital.

My point here is not to personalize the tutors' life histories but to call attention to how writing-center work is always involved in the making and remaking of the division of labor in contemporary society. As you read the essays within this volume, you will see the traces of class formation and reformation—and how these processes are enacted daily in writing centers. To my mind, this is what I would call the "politics of writing centers."

John Trimbur

Preface

This collection of essays addresses and critiques the politics of writing-center work. While a number of writing-center publications include essays on historical and theoretical perspectives on writing-center administration and tutoring, no collection to date focuses on and explores the terrain of power in which writing centers are located. This collection does not provide a manual on how to direct or tutor in a writing center. Nor does it catalogue the many (and well-founded) grievances writing center people have. Rather, the authors of the twelve chapters investigate sites of conflict and recommend directions for positive change.

This book is divided into two parts. In Part 1, "The Politics of Conversation," contributors explore the consequences of not only having identities constructed for and about writing centers by others, but also about the identities writing centers construct for themselves and in association with other campus communities. In keeping with the interventionist focus of the CrossCurrents series, authors point the way to new opportunities for productive reidentification. Authors in Part 1 also look at the political exchanges that happen during the course of writing-center work—personal, economic, and pedagogical. The authors investigate "talk" in writing centers: who engages in it, where the voices come from, and whose voices become privileged. The essays in this section discover and reveal opportunities for conversations with other voices in other places.

Peter Carino opens by reflecting on the conflicted relationships many writing centers have had with composition studies: writing centers have often adopted a posture of victimization yet have drawn on composition theory to justify their own pedagogy. Carino examines the ways in which this complicated situation can be publicly oppositional or locally amicable.

While Carino confronts the politics of identifying with the discipline of composition studies, Pat McQueeney and Katherine Fischer and Muriel Harris examine the politics of identifying with persistent writing-center metaphors. McQueeney tells a story that is both paradoxical and telling. In narrating her "paradigm drama" about the University of Kansas Writing Center, she shows how metaphors structure conceptual systems. Muriel Harris and Katherine Fischer go on to look at writing-center metaphors historically and contextually, arguing for multiple metaphors for multiple audiences.

Chapters 4 and 5 focus on power relationships in tutoring. Jane Cogie is interested in the ways writing centers can and do train tutors, both new and experienced, to deal with the real and uneven boundaries of ethically and pedagogically effective tutoring. She is particularly interested in the dilemma of avoiding oppression yet giving lower-achieving students the insider knowledge they need to succeed academically. Carrie Leverenz is interested in giving that insider knowledge to graduate students by creating the writing center as a site for them to perform their expertise in conversation with peer writers.

Chapters 6 and 7 broaden the political perspective by critiquing the economics of labor in the writing center. Linda Shamoon and Deborah Burns examine the notion of "the expert" in writing centers. They look into the relationship between the theoretical bases of writing centers and the kind of labor that gets performed and the kind of laborer who performs it. They recommend that centers shifting to a social perspective on the production of texts hire specialist tutors who will be, because of the nature of their work and the people with whom they work, nearer the political center of the university. Margaret Marshall closes out Part 1 by questioning the rhetorical prepositioning that leads to the invisibility of writing-center work in academic routines like hiring and tenure. She argues for a theoretical and political appraisal of the director's position within the disciplines of composition and writing centers.

In Part 2, "The Politics of Location," authors examine the material conditions of writing-center work. Contributors do not focus exclusively on the context of their individual institutions; rather, they study the architecture of power that supports and undermines writing-center work. Because writing centers must respond to changing paradigms in their institutions, the authors suggest ways that writing centers can be agents of their own change.

Carol Peterson Haviland, Carmen Fye, and Richard Colby open Part 2 with an examination of the options writing centers have for physical and administrative locations, charting the political implications of these choices. Pamela Childers and James Upton describe the contractual complexities and the unique decisions about personnel and space in secondary school writing centers.

Chapters 10 and 11 critically review the ways by which writing centers govern themselves. Eric Hobson and Kelly Lowe analyze the history and culture of the National Writing Centers Association (NWCA), especially in light of its rapid development and expansion, and they posit an agenda for the NWCA in the next decade. Jeanne Simpson and Barry Maid interrogate the writing-center community's resistance to establishing a formal accreditation procedure. The book closes with Christina Murphy and Joe Law's projection of radical changes for the academy and for writing centers in the twenty-first century. They identify several ways in which writing centers might respond to the challenge of educational outsourcing.

Considered in aggregate, the essays in this volume catalogue the political causes and consequences of writing-center traits that have long bothered the writing-center community. Writing-center work is heavily gendered. Because more women than men work in writing centers, the writing center is conceptualized in traditional feminine terms. The authors in this collection reveal the manifestations and results of the gendered writing center. They also scrutinize the political causes and effects of institutional marginalization, resulting once again from both material conditions and metaphorical or conceptual positioning. Readers of these essays will discover how writing-center professionals have, in the last two decades, performed academically valuable work and created a thriving professional community within some precarious institutional conditions.

At the same time the contributors find ways to celebrate writing-center success, they also accuse the writing-center community of complicity in sustaining the political conditions of marginalization. They find entry into the twenty-first century to signify the transition to a new stage for writing centers. Having performed the important "inside" work of establishing writing centers as sites for important intellectual work in educational institutions, the writing-center community now needs to take the next step of communicating to and connecting with broader political and intellectual audiences. The authors recommend, for instance, that writing-center professionals listen more carefully to the conversations of other disciplines, of upper administration, and of entities outside of the academy in order to become more politically competent in their work.

Because this book is in part a self-critique of writing centers, we feel obligated to share and critique our approach to putting this collection together. As coeditors, we conceptualized an overall vision of the book and chapter topics we thought should be covered. Then we used the NWCA membership roster to approach writing-center people whom we thought would be strong, potential contributors to the volume. Based on this list, we approached people whose work we knew, whose names we knew, whose CCCC, NWCA, or regional writing-center conference presentations we'd seen or heard about. We sent to these people a call for proposals and were delighted to receive so many

responses. Then we selected the proposals that best fit our chapter topics and the political thrust of the book.

One morning, we sat down to match authors' names and essay
titles with our envisioned chapter topics. When we finished, we
decided to examine the gender distribution of our contributors. During
this process, much to our shock and horror, we simultaneously realized
that although we were thinking about gender and writing centers, we
had never once—for a book about the politics of writing centers—
thought about including chapters on race or ethnicity or class in writing centers. It never once dawned on us, as we met over the course of
months of talking about this project, to consider the racial and economic politics of our own choice of topics and contributors. This
prompted us to give a presentation called "The Politics of Exclusion:
How Do We Think About Race and Class in the Profession?" at the
1999 NWCA meeting in Bloomington, Indiana. In it, we raised more
issues than we could answer, with questions like these:

- Who is not being represented in professional writing-center conversations?

- Who is doing the talking, and who's being talked about—and why
  do the answers bother us?

- Who attends the NWCA convention? Who participates in regional
  meetings and peer tutoring conferences? Who *doesn't* participate,
  and why? Whose voices remain unheard (or unheard of) in professional conversations?

- Who is drawn to the "discipline" of writing-center work, a subset
  of composition/rhetoric? And from this pool of practitioners, who
  has the funds and time to enter into the professional conversation?
  Whose voices are never heard because of the economic politics of
  their institutions and NWCA?

Ultimately, we suggested that the discipline is currently defined
nationally by those who participate in professional conversations (on
the WCenter listserv, at writing-center conferences, and in writing-
center publications). Thus, we realized that we, and probably many
other writing-center workers, have a restricted and exclusive notion of
what writing centers are and do, and what they can be in the future.
How can writing-center workers and professional entities (conferences and publications) be more proactive in encouraging the voices
of rarely heard writing-center directors and tutors whose experiences
are not part of the general conversation of writing centers? How can

the writing-center community use the resources available to it to be more inclusive?

If not answers, we have suggestions. For instance, instead of offering prize money for winners of the NWCA scholarship awards, we recommend providing awardees with a certificate and public recognition, and using the funds to assist tutors or directors from community colleges to travel to and present at NWCA meetings. We encourage writing-center periodicals to feature guest-edited issues by high school and community-college writing-center workers, by writing-center workers of color, or by workers who interact primarily with economically disadvantaged students. The NWCA Press could recruit a guest editor from an underrepresented group to assemble an edited collection specifically on the issue of race, gender, and/or class in writing centers.

What have we learned by thinking about our own blindness to what we believe are critical absences in writing-center publications and conversations? That one must always be on the lookout for what one isn't thinking of. That one must resist writing and speaking only to friends and colleagues in the profession. That one must *see,* and a way to begin doing that is by constantly thinking politically.

Acknowledgments

We wish to thank a number of friends and colleagues who have kept this project moving and organized: Emily Buller, Teresa Cole, Jody Cousins, Cheryl Hageman, Pepper Jo Six, and Elizabeth Snyder. They helped us find addresses, create mailing lists, keep track of disks and paper, and do the important fact checking for the book.

We also want to acknowledge friends and colleagues to whom we are indebted for their intellectual work at the University of Wyoming Writing Center, especially Peg Garner, Colin Keeney, Diane LeBlanc, Judy Powers, Cindy Wambeam, and Carolyn Young. These past and present colleagues in the Writing Center have passionately debated the politics of writing-center work at our own institution. Better yet, they have been willing to take on activist roles, changing the nature of the work all of us in the Writing Center and our writing-across-the-curriculum colleagues have performed.

The National Writing Centers Association, the Midwest Writing Centers Association, and the Rocky Mountain Writing Centers Association have been important to us because their meetings have given us the opportunity to speak about our own interest in politics and to hear what other folks have had to say.

Our colleagues in the University of Wyoming Center for Teaching Excellence (CTE)—Andy Bryson, Joe Gregg, Pat Hutchings, Audrey Kleinsasser, and Laurie Milford—have supported this project indirectly and directly through their technological know-how, their interest in the politics of education, and their collective great sense of humor. The CTE and Academic Affairs have also generously supported our travel to writing-center meetings. Our greatest debt is to Jim Wangberg, former director of the Center for Teaching Excellence. Everyone should have such a strong advocate.

Finally, we want to thank Charles Schuster, general editor of the CrossCurrents series, for his enthusiasm for this project and his wise editorial advice.

1

Writing Centers and Writing Programs

Local and Communal Politics

Peter Carino

No single political, pedagogical, or theoretical relationship exists collectively between writing centers and writing programs, for every relationship varies by local context—an idea currently potent in writing-center discourse. Nevertheless, writing-center and, to a lesser extent, composition scholarship identify various models, ranging from the center as a remedial supplement run by a director accorded less than full professional status, to the center as an independent campuswide facility for teaching writing, usually as the centerpiece in a writing-across-the-curriculum (WAC) program headed by an administrator or tenured faculty member. Midpoint on this continuum lies the center linked with an English department as writing-program complement, serving students in both composition and other courses, providing a home for a tenured faculty director, enjoying reasonable status in the institution, and sharing a theoretical perspective with the writing program.

These models certainly vary in practice. At one institution, a tenured faculty member may direct a supplemental center; at another, a campuswide WAC center may be located in an English department; or any model may be housed in a larger learning center. A glance at Paula Gillespie's *Directory of Writing Centers* (1999) suggests the myriad arrangements. Nevertheless, writing centers form a community unified by several factors: a national organization and several regional organizations that imply what centers should be; a desire for professional respectability in their relationships with writing programs (first-year composition or WAC); a body of scholarship that has often appropriated composition theory to explain center work or distance that work from classroom practice; and, perhaps most important, a

1

commitment to one-on-one instruction, often delivered by peers, whether addressing grammatical problems in a supplemental lab or discipline-specific notions of composing in a WAC center.

These shared characteristics define centers as a discipline, or at least an educational phenomenon, and determine their relationships with composition—professionally, theoretically, and pedagogically. These relationships have strongly contributed to the tensions haunting writing centers as they have struggled with the sting of marginalization and the desire for empowerment, driving them, individually and communally, to sometimes assume an adversarial stance toward composition programs and scholarship, yet sharing the same educational mission of teaching writing. I do not propose any "ideal" relationship as an alternative to those that have emerged; rather, I want to examine how writing-center relationships with composition programs and composition studies affect the construction of professional identity and the implementation of center practice in ways both energizing and debilitating.

The Center as Supplement

Though writing centers have varied in mission and practice, it is a commonplace of center and composition scholarship that many were established as remedial supplements to composition programs. More specifically, centers were to "carry the ball for mechanics" or to "give first aid to students," as Barbara Walvoord (1981) and Maxine Hairston (1982) respectively put it, much to the chagrin of Steven North in his oft-cited "The Idea of a Writing Center" (1984, 436). While North denounced these figurations, they typify the treatment of centers in composition scholarship, which was happy to assign them the current-traditional pedagogy it was repudiating in search of a process paradigm. Although some early centers were more than remedial supplements, early center scholarship illustrates that many accepted the supplemental role defined in Hairston's and Walvoord's portrayals. Betty MacFarland's 1975 description of a writing lab has often served center scholars as a ready example of complicity. MacFarland accepts without doubt that "mechanical correctness" is best taught in the lab—"the logical place for such supplementary instruction" (153).

MacFarland's essay is no anomaly, as early issues of the *Writing Lab Newsletter* attest. Robert L. Meredith (1978), at Georgia Tech, reports creating a departmental handbook so that "the faculty member can be sure that the information the lab gives out about a particular error he or she is especially concerned with will be 'correct'"(2). At Montgomery College, Myrna Goldenberg (1979) trumpets her center's success "in fulfilling the stated goal of support for the floundering freshman English student" (2). Toni Lopez (1979), at the University of Florida, describes a lab where students complete diagnostic modules before beginning tutorials "in the areas of grammatical and mechanical weaknesses indicated by their themes throughout the quarter" (5). Lopez's title, "Coordinating the Writing Lab with the Composition Program," implies equal footing, but her rhetoric unapologetically constructs the lab as a service to composition, designed to "meet the needs of students and aid the instructors effectively" (4). Though a supplemental mission invites marginalization, it can provide a secure albeit subjugated role on campus, and supplemental labs likely will continue to exist, maybe in greater proportion than the writing-center community would like to admit.

Irene Clark and Dave Healy (1996) attribute supplemental marginalization to pressure from the writing program to ensure that writing centers maintain an ethical relationship to students and instructors: "The emphasis on remedial education and on the mastery of grammar-based content was a 'safe' function for writing centers to assume because it was deemed by the academy an unfortunate but necessary supplement to the more important scholarly work that occurred in the classroom" (33). Clark and Healy cite this issue as the underlying motivation for the writing-center community's commitment to Rogerian nondirective tutoring, which they then critique. However, capitulation to a supplemental role likely originated as much from well-intended compliance in an amicable local relationship as from intimidation by writing programs.

Designated *labs,* many supplemental centers carried philological baggage associating them with science labs, which had always been (and remain) supplements to the classroom (see Russell 1991, 92–99, 247–49). Furthermore, the earliest writing labs originated from a classroom practice called the "laboratory method" (Carino 1995). Though this method often included much more than grammatical drill, the numerous labs set up to help basic writers admitted under open admissions initiatives of the 1970s would not have had recourse to that history. Thus, many labs likely accepted a supplementary role to create a space for themselves programmatically and pedagogically as a helpmate to the writing program, itself adjusting to open admissions and the so-called paradigm shift to process instruction. Theoretically, with little center scholarship to suggest other possibilities, such labs accepted current traditionalism. Add the probable funding constraints to both writing programs and labs, the pressure to help basic writers succeed, and the lack of full professional status for many directors, and it is logical that center scholarship included essays promulgating a supplemental mission.

Supplementation fostered an image of centers as writing-program housewives. Even by 1988, Gary Olson and Evelyn Ashton-Jones' survey of writing-program directors' perceptions of center directors laments that "a substantial number of the respondents" referred to the center directors as "she" and constructed them in terms of "a kind of *wife*" (emphasis original), with one even recommending that they "provide chocolate chip cookies to writing center clients" (24). A scant few years ago, Dave Healy's study of director demographics (1995b) reports that 74 percent are female, 40 percent hold a Ph.D., and less than half (46 percent) have tenure-track positions (30). In a sarcastic but insightful metaphor, Nancy Grimm (1996) sums up the sexism underlying Healy's data, complaining that writing centers "are supposed to make due with what they have, to keep the home tidy, and put a perky ribbon in their hair when visitors come" (532).

Grimm's acerbic wit underscores a critique in which she charges even centers today with playing the role of housewife, teaching students the good manners they need to succeed in the classroom. She argues that although centers have moved beyond grammar drill, they collude with writing programs in enforcing institutionally rewarded discourse conventions that ignore the subject positions students bring from their home cultures in favor of those of the mainstream. In one sense, this criticism is unfair, for Grimm speaks from a position of power in the very mainstream she denounces, and like it or not, students, by their very presence, demonstrate a desire, albeit sometimes conflicted, to enter the mainstream. Nevertheless, Grimm's argument bears upon the supplemental relationship of centers to writing programs as well as other campus entities. For early labs, supplementation was a means of survival, while pedagogically, with a lack of scholarship to guide them, they were probably doing what they could as best they could, figuring it out, so to speak. In contrast, today's writing centers, with all due respect for the literacy politics Grimm cites, have made much progress in determining their relationship to writing programs and entities beyond them, "colluding" to expand their pedagogy and influence on campus. This expansion requires a degree of supplementation, as even powerful WAC centers "supplement" writing instruction across disciplines. However, in forging WAC relationships, centers have redefined supplementation as a means to empowerment rather than as capitulation to a marginal position in the writing program. But not without a new set of problems.

Beyond Supplementation:
Leaving Composition Programs

The antithesis to supplemental centers is succinctly profiled by Joyce Kinkead and Jeannette Harris in their introduction to *Writing Centers in Context* (1993):

> Successful programs establish relationships in host environments that are best described as interactive—the writing center shapes its context as well as being shaped by it. For example, on many campuses writing centers have significantly influenced pedagogy throughout the curriculum. Peer editing, collaborative learning, and computer technology—now commonplace in most writing courses—often originate in writing centers. Writing-across-the-curriculum programs also often evolve out of successful writing center programs and directly influence the way in which courses in every discipline are taught. (xvi)

This depiction demonstrates that centers are reshaping composition classes through collaborative pedagogy; it also suggests that writing centers' liaisons with WAC programs garner influence beyond composition programs.

How did centers reach this position? As composition scholarship began to question the efficacy of teaching grammar in isolation, few centers could have held to the mission set forth in essays such as Lopez's or MacFarland's, even had they wanted to. George Hillocks' metastudy (1986) of composing research found that grammar instruction in isolation actually impeded students' ability to write. Hillocks' work quantitatively corroborated the logic and influence of Mike Rose's arguments in "Remedial Writing Courses: A Critique and a Proposal" (1983), an essay contemporary with North's "Idea of a Writing Center" (1984) and serving as a similar call for recognition for basic writing. In such an environment, labs began to draw on composition scholarship to expand their own instructional offerings, to lay claim to a stake in the process paradigm, and to convince writing instructors of the soundness of their approach. Probably as equally influential as composition scholarship was the day-to-day experience of lab workers themselves, many of whom were composition instructors as well. Able to address rhetorical matters, many centers were already expanding their pedagogy and mission at the same time that accounts of supplemental labs were deemed acceptable for publication as definitions of writing centers.

Contemporary with essays accepting supplementation, others in early *Writing Lab Newsletter* issues were already suggesting the kinds of liaisons Kinkead and Harris adumbrate above. Just months after

Lopez's essay, Janice Neuleib (1980) touts a "multi-purpose center" at Illinois State serving "graduate students as well as the undergraduates" and "the English major who wants an 'A' instead of a 'B' in Chaucer as well as . . . the student in developmental English who just wants to stay in school" (3). Three issues later, Diana Freisinger (1980) chastises composition faculty who would define the center as remedial, arguing for an identity outside of the writing program and English department. In the inaugural issue of *The Writing Center Journal*, Muriel Harris and Kathleen Yancey (1980) assert, "Although the first mission of a new writing lab is usually to supplement or to be integrated into the freshman writing course, labs have begun to respond to the needs of writers throughout their college years" (40). They go on to discuss one program's placing lab tutors in classrooms and another's preparing prelaw students for the LSAT. That such essays shared space with those endorsing remedial supplementation indicates that although the writing-center community had a high tolerance for diverse missions, it quickly developed a low tolerance for marginalization. Essays accepting supplementation soon disappeared.

Throughout the 1980s and bolstered midpoint by North's "Idea," center scholarship continually called for expansion beyond the writing program. Surfacing regularly in the *Writing Lab Newsletter, The Writing Center Journal,* and in papers at regional conferences, essays in this vein form a corpus of what might be called "expansionist narratives" (see J. Harris 1982; M. Harris 1982; Simpson 1985; Baltrinic 1988; Besser 1990; Mullin 1990; Yahner and Murdick 1991). Expansionist narratives reached full steam in Ray Wallace and Jeanne Simpson's *The Writing Center: New Directions* (1991), the first anthology on writing centers published in nearly ten years. By its very title and with nearly all its contributors advocating outreach efforts, this collection signaled that by the 1990s writing centers were serving a variety of campus entities—from athletic to retention programs. Wallace's own piece goes so far as to renounce the term *lab*, explicitly associating it with willing submission to English departments, error hunting, bad staffing, and a punitive relationship to students. He aggressively argues that writing *centers* should ally themselves with units outside of English and composition to increase funding and status.

Though expanding their scope of influence, centers continued to appropriate composition scholarship to explain their work, while claiming equality with, and even superiority to, the classrooms of the writing program. Aside from North's grounding center work in process pedagogy, other essays in the 1980s recruited the collaborative pedagogy of Kenneth Bruffee (Warnock and Warnock 1984) and, later, social constructionism. Regarding the latter, Lisa Ede's "Writing as a Social Process: A Theoretical Foundation for Writing Centers" (1989) and Andrea Lunsford's "Collaboration, Control, and the Idea of a Writing Center" (1991) both argue that center work enacts the social constructionist theory then dominating composition scholarship. These essays sought theoretical alignment with composition and, by extension, program equality.

Occasionally such hopes resulted in a mutually productive relationship. As Mark Waldo (1990) reports, center and program could "share an equal and complementary relationship . . . linked philosophically, each grounded in a similar theoretical perspective from which their pedagogy stems" (73). But such détente proved the exception, for as centers expanded, their scholarship, as Thomas Hemmeter (1990) demonstrates, increasingly castigated and even vilified writing programs and instructors. Surveying numerous essays, Hemmeter traces what he called a "duality of discourse" that "inverts the hierarchy [with the writing program] to claim superiority over the classroom in some ways," portraying the center as "a place of nurture, in contrast to the classroom as a place of torture" (38). This tendency can be partly justified as a counterattack against marginalization, but in another sense center scholars were sinking to the ad hominem they detested in composition's view of the center as grammatical fix-it shop.

There is much in this dynamic of what postmodern and postcolonial theory recognize as the need for "the other." In common parlance, "the other" is anyone not like those in a bonded group (Linn 1996). Composition and writing-center scholars are both guilty of oppressing the other, the former by marginalizing center work, the latter by vilifying composition. A happier history might have occurred had centers and programs worked together to increase the professional status of both. On a few campuses, this has happened with the formation of departments of writing, but in most locales and in the community of professionals who teach writing, whether in centers or classrooms, the relationship between the two has proven profitable to neither. This need for the other can be partly explained by the underlying marginalization of institutional hierarchies. As composition began to assert itself as a discipline, it did so in the face of the division of composition and literature in English departments, with literature privileged (see Berlin 1996). In turn, despite expansion efforts, writing centers found and still often find themselves subjugated not only to literature but to composition—marginalized by the marginalized.

Beyond WAC: Institutional Alignment

Often failing to form an alliance with writing programs against the perceived oppression of literature, centers have increasingly recommended to one another not only increased WAC activity but also separation from English departments in exchange for affiliation with central administration in the service of the university mission.

In a 1994 article composed primarily of e-mail correspondence, Jeanne Simpson, Steve Braye, and Beth Boquet hash out the possible benefits and perils of such linkages. Simpson, a first-generation director who became a central administrator, urges her younger colleagues to embrace institutional goals, particularly student retention. Taking a conservative position opposite Grimm's (1996) radical call "to explore the contradictions in literacy work" (546), Simpson dismisses the notion of centers as politically subversive and heavily attributes marginal identity crises to center professionals themselves. Braye and, to a lesser extent, Boquet, fear institutional alignment might compromise their principles, holding to the outlaw identity the writing-center community has sometimes cultivated in response to marginalization. Simpson counters correctly that centers, despite their subversive posturing, are not outside the institution and that everyone in higher education sometimes faces "divergence between personal goals and the institution's announced goals" (70). While wise to renounce self-marginalizing notions of subversion, she oversimplifies Braye's reticence when she indicts the English department for his problems—lack of status, freedom, budget—and proposes affiliation with central administration as a ready solution.

While center directors may read Simpson's advice as a movement into WAC (and likely it includes those efforts), university administrators these days, as Simpson notes, are strongly interested in supporting anything that contributes to retention. Since at-risk, first-year writers are often the most difficult to retain, centers must recognize that retention means working with them as well as comfortably matriculated students in WAC courses. There is nothing wrong with working with basic writers, and centers have always been good at serving them. Furthermore, centers can win administrative favor if they can demonstrate that they contribute to retention. However, if center scholarship is representative, as writing centers have sought to expand their influence, basic writers have been left behind because they contribute to the marginalized image centers have been trying to escape. That is, it has become more prestigious in the writing-center community, and more publishable, to recount efforts of tutoring engineering students or law school candidates than basic writers—the very students at the core of institutional retention efforts.

Even when central administration encourages WAC efforts, difficulties arise. In the context of expansion, the writing program comes to mean far more than first-year composition. And if the writing program and English department faculty do not understand center work, directors may be fooling themselves to think other faculty more easily will. Granted, some who respect the center's expertise in teaching writing and admit their own lack will leave the center alone to work with students as it sees fit. Others are no less likely, and probably more likely, than composition instructors to see the center as an editing service, even willing to sacrifice the ethics of having students' papers corrected (something English teachers oppose) so that they themselves can read cleaner papers. This stance is not surprising given that faculty outside English commonly have their scholarship edited for grammatical and stylistic effectiveness by journal editors or paid freelancers. Further compounding the problem is the suspicion that a writing tutor outside the discipline can do little more than correct errors and the assumption that teaching writing is not the job of all disciplines. Certainly center directors can educate these faculty, but the task will be more difficult than working with composition instructors.

Even assuming that centers can maintain professional status while working in retention efforts, even assuming they can surmount the obstacles posed by WAC, trying to serve all students requires resources. As North first argued in his "Idea" (1984), writing centers should not engage in efforts beyond talking to writers one-to-one "like some marginal ballplayer—by doing whatever it takes to stay on the team" (446). North extends this argument ten years later in his "Revisiting 'The Idea of a Writing Center'" (1994). Though acknowledging the timeliness of "Idea," he repudiates it as "romantic idealization" and calls for stronger alliances with composition courses, "bringing center and classroom, tutoring and teaching into this tighter orbit" (16). North recognizes that this less ambitious arrangement will not "achieve perfect harmony" with the writing program but that problems will "not be dissipated through the bureaucratic structures of a large campus" (17). Ultimately he endorses, at least for his own center, connecting "the Writing Center to our Writing Sequence through the English major" (17).

North's return home to English elicited much criticism in the writing-center community, with disappointment and even feelings of betrayal expressed on WCenter, the community's online discussion group. In print, Cynthia Haynes-Burton, in a 1995 letter to *The Writing Center Journal,* censures North for "sounding a cynical and defeatist alarm" (181), denouncing what she sees as his assumption that a center's success should be measured by its relationship to the writing program. North (1995), in rebuttal, argues that he would be willing to expand only if financial and personnel resources were made available but holds to his position that when the center "seeks to meet a broad array of institutional needs—to become all things to all people—it runs a considerable risk of being of limited value to anyone" (185). North's position foregrounds the political complexity of local context, and given this complexity, the writing-center community has increasingly agreed that context powerfully contributes to determining the writing center's relationship with the writing program, whether defined as basic writing, first-year writing, WAC, or more.

Conclusion: A Room of One's Own?

The call to respect context in writing-center scholarship has more of an impact on local program relationships than on the community's professional status as a whole. As a community, writing centers have enjoyed remarkable growth in their national and regional organizations; the two journals dedicated to center work have flourished; several collections of essays such as this one have appeared; and the National Writing Centers Association (NWCA) has established its own press. In addition, recognizing that centers and classrooms have the same objectives but address them differently, center scholarship increasingly prefers to find its own way rather than always explaining its pedagogy through composition theory.

Regarding program relations, however, the community remains conflicted. As Muriel Harris' lead essay in the tenth-anniversary issue of *The Writing Center Journal* argues in 1990, "It is a truism of this field that writing centers tend to differ from one another because they have evolved within different kinds of institutions and different programs and therefore serve different needs" (15). Harris' essay set the tone for the remainder of the decade. In 1993, Joyce Kinkead and Jeannette Harris, despite their powerful definition of a center cited earlier, assure readers of their *Writing Centers in Context* that "it is [centers'] environment, academic and otherwise, that most directly shapes them" (xv). Dave Healy concurs, recommending that centers "celebrate our differences and affirm our commonalities" (1995a, 24). Bobbie Silk, in her introduction to *The Writing Center Resource Manual* (1998), tells readers, "Without having been coached to do so, every contributor to this manual makes clear in his or her article that writing centers are individual and contextual" (I.1).

This commitment to local context is a healthy development, countering political calls such as Grimm's for radical positioning, programmatic advice such as Simpson's for institutional alignment, or theoretical arguments such as Ede's and Lunsford's calls to embrace social constructionism, for it respects the diverse obstacles individual centers face: funding, admissions standards, and attitudes toward writing instruction. Further, it delivers centers from a communal ideology based on continual expansion, by which the once colonized becomes colonizer. In the contextual ideology of the 1990s, every center has a room of its own in the writing-center community, though the size and decor may differ in relation to individual writing programs on individual campuses.

This stance has curiously emerged simultaneously with the community's desire for some kind of system of writing-center accreditation, first expressed in a proposal by Joe Law at the first NWCA National Conference in 1994 (see Law 1995), and subsequently in the NWCA Board's appointment of a subcommittee on the issue and discussions of it at the Board's sessions at the Conference on College Composition and Communication (CCCC). Accreditation implies consensus, so even if local context is respected, as Law advocates, accreditation may determine where the furniture goes (and much more) in each center's room of its own. While accreditation might become a force for empowering writing centers in their relationships with the writing program and the institution, pressuring both to acknowledge the center's place in educating students, it raises vexing questions that the writing-center community might find difficult to reconcile with respect for local context. What should the director's status be? Whom should the center serve and in what numbers? What kind of instruction should the center deliver? Asking these questions generates productive dialogue, but answering them is another matter, as was evident at the 1999 NWCA Conference, where the Board voted to postpone implementation of an accreditation program. Moreover, these questions are just few of the many that will continue not only to confound accreditation efforts but also the place of individual writing centers in relation to individual writing programs, the writing-center community in relation to the composition community, and individual writing centers in relation to one another. Whatever the local context, the center's relationship to the writing program will remain a challenge constantly refigured and negotiated, and well it should be. To have it otherwise would lead to a stagnancy entrapping the community in, as Frederic Jameson (1983) puts it, "the anticipation of a collectivity which has not yet come into being" (286). And probably never will.

Works Cited

Baltrinic, B. 1988. "Extending the Writing Center." *Writing Lab Newsletter* 13 (1): 4–7.

Berlin, J. 1996. *Rhetorics, Poetics, and Cultures: Refiguring English Studies.* Urbana, IL: NCTE.

Besser, M. P. 1990. "The Writing Center: A Center for All Disciplines." In *Voices of Empowerment: Proceedings of the 1989 Eleventh Annual ECWCA Conference,* edited by L. Masiello, 182–86. Indiana, PA: A.G. Halldin.

Carino, P. 1995. "Early Writing Centers: Toward a History." *The Writing Center Journal* 15 (2): 103–15.

Clark, I. L., and D. Healy. 1996. "Are Writing Centers Ethical?" *WPA: Writing Program Administration* 20 (1/2): 32–48.

Ede, L. 1989. "Writing as a Social Process: A Theoretical Foundation for Writing Centers." *The Writing Center Journal* 9 (2): 3–13.

Freisinger, D. 1980. "Stretch the Lab." *Writing Lab Newsletter* 4 (10): 6–7.

Gillespie, P. 1999. *Directory of Writing Centers.* New Berlin, WI: Metagraphix.

Goldenberg, M. 1979. "The Evolution of a Writing Center." *Writing Lab Newsletter* 4 (1): 2–4.

Grimm, N. 1996. "Rearticulating the Work of the Writing Center." *College Composition and Communication* 47 (4): 523–48.

Hairston, M. 1982. "The Winds of Change: Thomas Kuhn and the Revolution in the Teaching of Writing." *College Composition and Communication* 33 (1): 76–88.

Harris, J. 1982. "Redefining the Role of the Writing Center." *Writing Lab Newsletter* 7 (3): 1–2.

Harris, M. 1982. "Growing Pains: The Coming of Age of Writing Centers." *The Writing Center Journal* 2 (1): 1–8.

———. 1990. "What's Up and What's In: Trends and Traditions in Writing Centers." *The Writing Center Journal* 11 (1): 15–25.

Harris, M., and K. B. Yancey. 1980. "Beyond Freshman Comp: Expanded Uses of the Writing Lab." *The Writing Center Journal* 1 (1): 41–48.

Haynes-Burton, C. 1995. "Letter." *The Writing Center Journal* 15 (2): 181–83.

Healy, D. 1995a. "In the Temple of the Familiar: The Writing Center as Church." In *Writing Center Perspectives,* edited by B. L. Stay, C. Murphy, and E. Hobson, 12–25. Emmitsburg, MD: NWCA Press.

———. 1995b. "Writing Center Directors: An Emerging Portrait of the Profession." *WPA: Writing Program Administration* 18 (3): 26–43.

Hemmeter, T. 1990. "The 'Smack of Difference': The Language of Writing Center Discourse." *The Writing Center Journal* 11 (1): 35–48.

Hillocks, G. 1986. *Research on Written Composition: New Directions for Teaching.* Urbana, IL: National Conference on Research in English, ERIC Clearinghouse on Reading and Communication Skills, National Institute of Education (available through NCTE).

Jameson, F. 1983. *The Political Unconscious: Narrative as a Socially Symbolic Act.* London: Routledge.

Kinkead, J. A., and J. G. Harris, eds. 1993. *Writing Centers in Context: Twelve Case Studies.* Urbana, IL: NCTE.

Law, J. 1995. "Accreditation and the Writing Center: A Proposal for Action." In *Writing Center Perspectives,* edited by B. L. Stay, C. Murphy, and E. Hobson, 155–61. Emmitsburg, MD: NWCA Press.

Linn, R. 1996. *A Teacher's Introduction to Postmodernism.* Urbana, IL: NCTE.

Lopez, T. 1979. "Coordinating the Writing Lab with the Composition Program." *Writing Lab Newsletter* 4 (1): 4–7.

Lunsford, A. 1991. "Collaboration, Control, and the Idea of a Writing Center." *The Writing Center Journal* 12 (1): 3–10.

MacFarland, B. 1975. "The Non-Credit Writing Laboratory." *Teaching English in the Two-Year College* 1 (3): 153–54.

Meredith, R. L. 1978. "The Departmental Handbook." *Writing Lab Newsletter* 3 (10): 1–2.

Mullin, J. 1990. "Empowering Ourselves: New Directions for the Nineties." *Writing Lab Newsletter* 14 (10): 11–13.

Neuleib, J. 1980. "Proving We Did It." *Writing Lab Newsletter* 4 (7): 2–4.

North, S. 1984. "The Idea of a Writing Center." *College English* 46 (5): 433–46.

———. 1994. "Revisiting 'The Idea of a Writing Center.'" *The Writing Center Journal* 15 (1): 7–19.

———. 1995. "Letter." *The Writing Center Journal* 15 (2): 183–85.

Olson, G., and E. Ashton-Jones. 1988. "Writing Center Directors: The Search for Professional Status." *WPA: Writing Program Administration* 12 (1/2): 19–28.

Rose, M. 1983. "Remedial Writing Courses: A Critique and a Proposal." *College English* 45 (2): 109–28.

Russell, D. 1991. *Writing in the Academic Disciplines, 1870–1990: A Curricular History.* Carbondale, IL: Southern Illinois University Press.

Silk, B. B., ed. 1998. *The Writing Center Resource Manual.* Emmitsburg, MD: NWCA Press.

Simpson, J. H. 1985. "What Lies Ahead for Writing Centers: Position Statement on Professional Concerns." *The Writing Center Journal* 5 (2): 35–39.

Simpson, J., S. Braye, and B. Boquet. 1994. "War, Peace, and Writing Center Administration." *Composition Studies/Freshman English News* 22 (1): 65–95.

Waldo, M. 1990. "What Should the Relationship Between the Writing Center and Writing Program Be?" *The Writing Center Journal* 11 (1): 73–80.

Wallace, R. 1991. "Sharing the Benefits and Expense of Expansion: Developing a Cross-Curricular Cash Flow for a Cross-Curricular Writing Center." In *The Writing Center: New Directions,* edited by R. Wallace and J. Simpson, 82–101. New York: Garland.

Wallace, R., and J. Simpson, eds. 1991. *The Writing Center: New Directions.* New York: Garland.

Walvoord, B. 1981. *Helping Students Write Well: A Guide for Teachers in All Disciplines*. New York: MLA.

Warnock, T., and J. Warnock. 1984. "The Liberatory Writing Center." In *Writing Centers: Theory and Administration,* edited by G. Olson, 16–23. Urbana, IL: NCTE.

Yahner, W., and W. Murdick. 1991. "The Evolution of a Writing Center: 1972–1990." *The Writing Center Journal* 11 (2): 13–28.

2

What's in a Name?

Pat McQueeney

Writing support at the University of Kansas began in 1985 with this proclamation by a faculty task force: "The Writing Center will initiate and coordinate activities to improve student writing by means of helping teachers to assign and handle writing in the most efficient and pedagogically effective ways" (Task Force 1985, 3). Only a year before, the task force had circulated drafts of a proposal for a traditional student-writing service, which they called the *KU Writing Center* (Task Force 1984). The focus of writing support changed over the year, however, from students to teachers. Faculty requested redirection of the proposed service to "help faculty and graduate assistants cope with student writing needs" rather than with direct intervention with students ("Faculty" 1984, 1). In response to faculty interest, this new unit became a writing-across-the-curriculum (WAC) consulting service for faculty interested in incorporating writing into their teaching.

For fifteen years the Writing Center at the University of Kansas promoted both writing for learning and writing in the disciplines through individual and departmental consultations, faculty workshops, and a website for faculty. In addition, the staff collaborated with faculty to provide discipline- and course-specific support to students. Some of the efforts to support students included designing assignments and class-specific supplemental materials, giving class presentations and voluntary enhancement sessions, and maintaining a student website with more than one hundred original documents. For ten years, the office staff also provided limited tutoring for students of clients; however, this tutoring was course specific and did not, therefore, constitute a true writing center. Tutoring services ceased when it became apparent that the limited tutoring was compromising opportunities to receive funding for a full-service writing center.

Despite not being a true writing center, the *Writing Center* as a name made sense to enthusiastic faculty seeking to make the service the center of writing initiatives on campus. No doubt the linguists in the group understood what George Lakoff and Mark Johnson describe as the power of metaphors to structure "our conceptual system and the kinds of everyday activities we perform" (1980, 145). The task force was overly optimistic, however. As with most start-up services, this one wasn't at the *center* of anything philosophically, pedagogically, or politically. Neither was it *a* center in the sense of being a place of research. Nor was it a *writing* center in the traditional understanding of a student-support service. Despite the well-intentioned effort of the task force, their decision to use a term that holds a well-established conventional meaning to create a new concept has confused perceptions of the scope and function of writing support at KU for fifteen years. Though the saga of the KU Writing Center is unique in some ways, the naming of this office demonstrates the power of names to shape conceptual systems—for worse and for better.

The nature of metaphors is at the root of this confusion. The task force had turned *writing center*, a conventional metaphor to use Lakoff and Johnson's term, into a "new" metaphor (1980, 139, 145). Writing specialists, however, know that this term is far from new. The metaphor, which the task force hoped to use to introduce a new concept—a writing service that worked through faculty in all disciplines to affect student writing—was already conventionalized. Many faculty and students were familiar with the conventional meaning of the term, having used writing centers at nearby community colleges. Not surprisingly, they were irritated when the KU Writing Center did not provide a range of services comparable to what they had expected from their prior experiences of writing centers. As recently as 1998 a respondent to an institutional-review survey about the quality of service wrote a scathing comment criticizing the fact that the WAC service did not tutor her students, even though the scope of the office's mandate was clearly identified on the survey. The name also camouflaged several contributions the WAC service could make to support faculty. Faculty aware of the conventional use of the phrase did not think of the Writing Center as a service for them. When staff had to refuse service to students while not being able to attract faculty, credibility was damaged. The mix of new and conventional metaphors damaged relations with potential users, confused the service's position within the larger institution, and complicated professional associations. Most significant, it delayed the establishment of a "real" student writing center.

Administrators also had preconceptions about the unit because of its name. The task force had successfully placed the service with the influential Academic Affairs office (now Office of the Provost), but the use of the word *center* raised caution within the administration. *Center* signifies more than place, as the founders recognized in their 1985 report. The Writing Center was to be a central point "in which the University's writing improvement will be focused," the task force had contended (3). The Kansas Board of Regents reiterated the political volatility of the term when it established guidelines in a policies and procedures manual for the use of *center* in the title of a unit (1995, 5D). At issue is the concern that an institution could be pressured to fund a project simply because it has the authoritative *center* in its name. At KU, university-level permission is now required to officially call a unit a center (Johnson 1999).

Although administrators were sensitive to the political volatility of the Writing Center as a new metaphor, for many years the same individuals were oblivious to the conventional use of the term. Staff scrupulously said *center* when identifying the office formally or when referring to writing-center services generally, but administrators consistently shifted the terminology to *lab* or *clinic*. Perhaps the student-support connotations of the word conjured up memories of student labs and clinics from their own school days. Unfortunately, while *writing lab* would succeed in communicating the general concept of a writing service for students, the Writing Center wasn't such a service. In addition, *lab* and *clinic* carry additional baggage that clouds the message about the nature of a faculty-development WAC service. As Peter Carino has noted, both terms tend to connote a medicinal metaphor, though *lab* is slightly more positive in that it suggests exploration and experimentation as opposed to the diagnosis and treatment associated with *clinic* (1992, 39, 41). Such connotations would be detrimental to any service at KU because of long-established resistance to funding anything deemed remedial. For a faculty service, such an association would be doubly damaging: faculty would be insulted at suggestions that they needed treatment, and those faculty who used the service would risk being labeled as remedial by their evaluators. Fortunately, most of the faculty regarded the service as nonmedicinal; unfortunately, some administrators never lost the medical vocabulary.

In addition to complicating relations with the administration, the misleading moniker denied the office and staff members clear professional affiliations. In the 1980s KU's model was so innovative that the director at the time urged staff to work through professional forums to expand the writing-center concept to include WAC models such as KU's. The effort was not successful. Writing-center colleagues embraced the work because of the common commitment to writing, but they were not willing to move from the conventional definition of *writing center*. And, though the Writing Center was actually a WAC service, WAC colleagues were less interested in a consultation model than in their popular workshop and writing-intensive approaches. Staff members became involved in both forums, even while the unique model and the name made the KU Writing Center suspect to colleagues on both sides. As WAC and writing-center dialogues grew to complement each other, the staff gained the advantage of being able to engage in multiple conversations as a result of being the writing center that wasn't. There continued to be a need, though, to define the KU service in the negative at conferences—as what it was not—during its years as the Writing Center.

By the late 1980s the complications created by this name caused the director to request a name change. For nearly five years, the requests were denied. Why was there such a long wait for naming relief? I can only speculate, but over the years the KU Writing Center had become a convenient all-purpose title for writing support. The ambiguity created by the clash of the new and conventional forms of the term allowed individuals to make multiple meanings of the title. The fusion of the new and conventional metaphors let administrators parse the name of this tiny service to sound like a student writing service, a WAC service, a writing-intensive curriculum, a faculty-development initiative, or all of the above. Such parsing gave parents and donors assurance that writing needs were being met, though the staff was sure to feel the ramifications of the ungrounded assertions. After hearing engaging university representatives who were liberal with their promises of writing support for prospective students, parents blamed the Writing Center when the services were not available. More seriously, potential donors saw no need to endow a student-writing service after hearing university representatives suggest that such a service already existed.

The name lessened the likelihood that either the WAC service or a writing center would be endowed; it also complicated internal requests for funding. As WAC services grew, faculty made clear that their commitment to incorporating writing was constrained by the lack of direct support services for students. Their compelling argument for a writing center was difficult to articulate because of the name confusion. Over eight years, the staff wrote five proposals for student-writing support, each of which was challenged as a redundancy. The complaint was that there was no need for additional funding because KU already had the Writing Center. When the writers substituted *lab* or *clinic* to identify the request, the comment was that no funding was available for remedial purposes. The proposals were stymied not by the absence of shared terminology but by the lack of shared meaning for the term *writing center*.

What the best-articulated arguments could not achieve, institutional reorganization accomplished. When Academic Affairs changed its name to the Office of the Provost, administrators could no longer deny the request of the Writing Center. The KU Writing Center became Writing Consulting in 1995. The parent office had shifted from a descriptor of services (Academic Affairs) to a place (Office of the Provost), while the WAC service went the opposite direction: from a place that really wasn't (the Writing Center) to a descriptor that clearly indicated services (Writing Consulting). Still holding out hope that a writing center was in KU's future, the staff qualified *Writing Consulting* with *Faculty Resources*, thereby suggesting Writing Consulting: Student Resources. The name was too long, admittedly: campus software often conflated its characters. Some were uncomfortable with the abstract nature of the name: a bill arrived addressed to Writing Consulting Center and to Writing Consultants. Despite these problems, no one any longer confused the service with a tutoring site or a computer lab.

The changed name raised the visibility of Writing Consulting. Faculty recognized in the new title a service designed for them. Inquiries about services increased, especially from faculty who could relate to consulting either because they had employed consultants or were consultants themselves. Administrators also realized from the new name that this was a faculty-development service. In addition, the absence of *writing center* in the name highlighted the gaps in the school's writing support. Faculty, students, and parents looking for a student writing center no longer saw the Writing Center listed in the campus directory, and questions about the absence of a student service increased.

Visibility was important, but it came at the cost of vulnerability. For all the problems the former name had caused, it had afforded a certain security: mere existence as the Writing Center served a purpose for university public relations. Now, school representatives no longer had the unit with the catchall name for their every writing reference. The absence of *writing center* in the name and the presence of an abstract title increased scrutiny of the office. To the benefit of the unit, the scrutiny led to the reporting line's being changed to the provost in charge of faculty development. As a faculty-development unit, however, Writing Consulting had to prove that services were not redundant to those offered through the newly opened Center for Teaching Excellence.

Renaming had complicated political positioning on campus and jeopardized the future of the service, but it made available terminology with which to articulate the proposal for a writing center. Within a year of the name change to Writing Consulting, the sixth proposal for a student writing center was accepted. The student service opened its doors

in fall of 1998. Several factors contributed to the success of this proposal, with the name change playing a significant role. The absence of
the Writing Center made obvious to the KU community that it did not
have student writing support. Moreover, because advocates could now
use *writing center* unambiguously as a conventional metaphor, the discourse was clearer. In addition, colleagues at a regional writing-center
conference helped the staff expand the proposal vocabulary. To com-
pensate for the medicinal connotations of *lab* and *clinic,* they substituted words such as *learning communities* that would connect to
current university themes (McQueeney 1997, 13–16).

Of course, when the writing center was funded, it couldn't be
called the Writing Center immediately. With the depths of KU bureaucracy, traces of the original name would remain attached to the faculty
WAC service as long as it existed. And official approval would be
required for the formal incorporation of *center* into the title. Most
important, after years of the confusion about the function of the Writing Center, as the newly appointed director of Writing Consulting I
thought it was important to launch the new service with a fresh identity. After all, since 1985 people had heard that KU did not have a writing center. The writing-center initiative risked becoming victim of its
parent unit's own name and publicity.

To clarify the affiliation between the two components of Writing
Consulting, the official title of the student service was *Writing Consulting: Student Resources.* Many of its student initiatives could
remain unidentified, but its tutoring services needed a distinctive name.
Michele Eodice, the writing-center coordinator, sought a student-
friendly title as she set about naming the multiple tutoring sites that
would span the campus. KU's distinctive and well-known mascot, the
Jayhawk, came to the rescue. Working from the concept of this myth-
ical, feisty bird, Eodice christened the tutoring offices Writer's Roosts,
used the slogan "Look for the Writer's Roosts!" to promote the numerous sites (six the first semester), and created a visual metaphor in the
logo of a Jayhawk roosting on a pencil.

The process of naming these sites had its own political hurdles: she
needed my approval to select the name and the approval of the intercollegiate licensing office to use the Jayhawk. In addition, we thought
it politically expedient to gain the associate provost's approval for both
this new metaphor and its visual representation. The Writer's Roosts
and the "Writing Jayhawk" logo are hits with the administration, students, and faculty. The connotations of *roost* promote the center sites
as hangouts and student haunts, and few would equate a roost with a
computer lab. In fact, faculty and administrators are substituting *roosts*
in their lexicons for labs and clinics. With the medicinal metaphor less

frequently used, *writing center* is actually becoming the generic term of preference for a student-tutoring service. Finally, in the Writer's Roosts, KU has its writing center.

Its parent WAC service, however, no longer exists. Soon after its name changed and as the writing center opened, Writing Consulting: Faculty Resources came under institutional review for the first time in thirteen years. The review was never completed. The office was funded for an additional two years after preliminary feedback indicated that clients were highly satisfied with the work; nevertheless, the long-term prospects for Faculty Resources were unclear because of the lack of institutionalized commitment to writing. I had been the only WAC specialist on campus, so Writing Consulting: Faculty Resources closed in June 1999 when I departed for a faculty position at a nearby community college.

Ironically, the closing of Writing Consulting: Faculty Resources created yet more naming problems, but it provided opportunities as well. Writing Consulting: Student Resources became a truly cumbersome name for the remaining component of Writing Consulting, given the absence of its counterbalancing faculty office. The Writer's Roosts have proved to be well named, especially for the targeted student audience; however, a more formal name seemed to be necessary to appeal to school bureaucrats and potential funding sources. Fortunately, the closing of the WAC service marked the end of the confusion attached to the original name. The end of Writing Consulting: Faculty Resources opened up the opportunity—with a few bureaucratic discussions—for an unambiguous use of the name the *Writing Center*. Fifteen years after a student writing center was originally proposed, the name came full circle. In 1999 administration authorized the current service for students to operate with the official title of the *KU Writing Center* (Eodice 2001). At long last, the new and conventional metaphors could become one: name and function of the service now match. With the formal name change, students, faculty, and administrators all agree that they have a writing center at the University of Kansas.

Works Cited

Carino, P. [1992] 1995. "What Do We Talk About When We Talk About Our Metaphors: A Cultural Critique of Clinic, Lab and Center." In *Landmark Essays on Writing Centers,* edited by C. Murphy and J. Law, 37–46. Davis, CA: Hermagoras.

Eodice, M. 2001. KU Writing Center Director. Telephone interview by author. 9 March.

"Faculty Offer 'Sensitive' Advice to Writing Group." 1984. *Oread* [University of Kansas] 9, no. 13 (30 November): 1.

Johnson, J. 1999. Office of the Provost Representative. Interview with author, 22 January.

Kansas Board of Regents. 1995. "Centers, Institutes, and Bureaus." *Policies and Procedures Manual*, 5D.

Lakoff, G., and M. Johnson. 1980. *Metaphors We Live By*. Chicago: University of Chicago Press.

McQueeney, P. 1997. "Proposing a Writing Center: Experts' Advice." *Writing Lab Newsletter* 22 (3): 13–16.

Task Force on Writing Across the Curriculum. 1984. "Draft Proposal for a KU Writing Center." Lawrence, KS: University of Kansas.

Task Force on Writing Across the Curriculum. 1985. "Report." Lawrence, KS: University of Kansas.

3

Fill 'er Up, Pass the Band-Aids, Center the Margin, and Praise the Lord

Mixing Metaphors in the Writing Lab

Katherine M. Fischer and Muriel Harris

To the Beach

Like rivers flooding in spring, metaphors about writing centers rise up all the time, resisting attempts to sandbag them. They surface in how writing centers are described and how the writing process is viewed. They rise up in the language of directors and tutors, of colleagues and college presidents. They bubble up in the names applied to those who work in them as well as in the names used to identify such places. For close to two decades, metaphors have been applied to writing centers with unwavering variation. How valid are the writing-center metaphors in common currency? What do they say about how the world sees writing centers and responds to what writing centers think they see? How accurately do the metaphors encapsulate the views of who writing-center people think they are and how their writing centers are defined? To what degree do these metaphors affect the politics of writing centers' positions within the larger institutions?

Quicksand

A particularly useful examination of the metaphors writing centers resist includes those compiled by Michael A. Pemberton (1992), who explores ways in which writing centers are seen as prisons and hospitals. The writing center as prison is a place of student punishment for committing linguistic crimes (12). Like most criminals caged behind bars, students caught in this perspective are passive, hostile, or uncooperative, and their tutors, who cannot easily create an atmosphere of trust and cooperation, are jailers keeping writers at chain-gang drills and revisions. Teachers are the metaphoric judges who have no responsibility for writing difficulties, except to detect them—and to sentence writers to the writing center. The act of writing, itself, is reduced to something deserving of penal action, something to be corrected until it fits the stencil of societal mores. Only then is the student released and freed from further visits to the writing center. Prison as a metaphor has a bloody double edge; it limits the focus on what writing centers can do by emphasizing correction of sentence-level errors, and it inhibits tutors from seeing their *prisoners* as the writers they really are, capable of collaborative dialogue and discussion.

Another of Pemberton's metaphors—writing centers as hospitals—reveals the center as that place where students come with diseased texts. Tutors diagnose the nature of the problem, work on curing the helpless writer, and in doing so, quickly fall into the role of healers of sick and injured drafts (Purcell 1998, 3). Like doctors who are considered inept when patients don't respond to treatment or are sued for not prescribing the right treatment, writing centers become liable for students who don't recover and write acceptable texts. This medical metaphor also, of course, implies a movement from original health to disease to recovery, totally distorting the real growth and development of writers. The writing center as ER rushes the tutoring-learning process into even faster treatment, the one tutorial that will cure all. Here tutors and clients "race against time to sew up gaping voids of syntax or meaning and quickly knock some life back into the paragraphs" (Purcell 1998, 1), a scene all too familiar to far too many tutors—a scene that might play out in a tutor's mind as follows when she recognizes what is expected but not possible:

> Recently arrived on campus from Puerto Rico, Maria rubs her arms against the chill Midwestern fall afternoon. "Can somebody fix this?" she asks as she holds her hand over the paragraph on her paper as though it is bleeding. "I know the English is just so sick." She wants me to reach for the scalpel pencil. She believes my surgery will reattach the joint, reconnect the heart, and resuscitate her writing.

A related way of envisioning the work of tutors is casting them as midwives, as Donna Fontanarose Rabuck (1995) suggests. The tutor's role here is to use her expertise to nurture the birthing of voice. Unlike the doctor who will intervene and perhaps use manipulation to control the baby's birth, the midwife assists in a holistic, noninvasive way. In Rabuck's center, created to assist minority and economically disadvantaged students, tutorial work embraces attitudes of helping and mentoring rather than of fixing.

A variation of the tutor's role as mender of texts is the tutor as gas station attendant. The language in this metaphor shifts from blood veins to fuel lines and from heartbeat to the engine's hum. Students trained to be passive in the classroom, according to Cheryl Krapohl

(1989), see the center as "a service station . . . bring in your assignment and we'll tune 'er right up, reducing the tutor to a 'mechanic' in the conveyer-belt world of academia" (9). While medical and gas station metaphors might carry positive images of compassionate specialists— and tutors do value their caring role—writing problems are again conceived of as illnesses or mechanical failures, thereby firmly positioning the writing center in the world of remedial work. Moreover, such images too easily give way to the language of war, as Susan Sontag (1978) points out. When tutors as doctors fight disease, they are engaged in battle wiping out the enemy—poor comma use, hasty generalizations, and battalions of bad grammar. The foot soldier writer draws upon a trusty red pencil to eradicate the foe as commanded by the lieutenant tutor. Either way, as student soldiers or tutor healers, there's bloodshed on the page when the session is over.

Seeing the hospital and prison metaphors as self-fulfilling negative prophecies, Pemberton (1992) calls for changing writing-center metaphors to more benign ones—*workshops* and *studios*—to suggest the craftlike nature of tutorial work, or *centers* to enhance the image of gathering places for people and information. Like Pemberton's preference for studio writing centers, Andrea Lunsford (1991) advocates viewing the center as a Burkean parlor. Here, where successful collaboration is attained, the "notion of knowledge as always contextually bound" reigns. Lunsford acknowledges that such a center challenges the institution "that insists on rigidly controlled individual performance, on evaluation as punishment, on isolation" (8–9). Lunsford's Burkean parlor center thus pits the center against the institution, pushing it out of the center and into an oppositional stance— one that poses a threat to the status quo in higher education. And such a center firmly sandbags writing-center theorizing by containing it totally within the social construction framework, despite repeated arguments that writing centers operate under no single unifying theoretical approach (e.g., Hobson 1994; Murphy 1994). While Lunsford's parlor banishes the role of tutor as doctor (the current-traditional approach in which information about accepted academic forms is delivered to students so that they can fix or "heal" the text), it also denies the tutor as midwife (the expressivist approach in which the tutor helps students who, as writers, possess the needed internal knowledge and are only assisted in the process of making meaning in their writing).

Although the Burkean parlor writing center shifts writing centers to the margins, Carol Severino's (1994) writing center as borderland or contact zone positions writing centers not out on the margins or at the institutional center, but in some meeting ground "where different cultures, languages, literacies, and discourses 'meet, clash, and grapple with one another.' The center is a 'disciplinary borderland' where the rhetorics of the humanities, social sciences, and natural sciences meet—to both intersect and conflict" (2), producing a contact dialect somewhere between student talk and teacher talk. John R. Edlund (1994) notes the political value of this cushioning:

> I have been thinking about the writing center as a sort of buffer. When students come in really bothered and frustrated by the Writing Proficiency exam, we calm them down, give them strategies, try to increase self-esteem, etc. These are good things to do for the individual, but they also protect the system from hostile energy that might otherwise be directed toward office sit-ins and picket signs and nasty letters to the editor. In a practical way I know that one of the reasons that we are funded from year to year is for this buffering effect.

On the Sandbar

Just as the centers are constructed by those who shape them, people in writing centers debate the most controversial metaphor that continually protrudes into conversations—the perennial lab/center debate. Is this place a *lab* or a *center*? From a historical perspective, Peter Carino (1992) eliminates the *clinic*, a commonly used term in the early 1970s that was appropriate in sociopolitical terms for the open-admissions students pouring into higher education. The writing center as clinic, explains Carino, was based in a misguided humanitarianism (help those poor inadequate students) and in a tacit reactionary politics (make them write like us). But the clinic metaphor didn't last long before moving on to *lab*. When Carino examines the metaphor of lab, he finds it developing alongside a paradigm shift in composition to writing as process: "Those working in labs probably perceived their efforts in the connotation of lab as a place to experiment, to pose questions, and to seek solutions to problems" (35).

While Carino concludes that the lab metaphor contributed to the marginalization of writing centers, he asserts finally that the lab metaphor still works for some places but is rejected by others:

> The idea of experimentation and innovation, multiple possibility and productive chaos, which informed the metaphor for those who chose to call their enterprises labs, persists today as many of them have largely succeeded in maintaining this sense in the praxis of their labs as microcultures. For this reason, I believe, the lab metaphor has not gone the way of the clinic metaphor. Still, for those who read the metaphor pejoratively, it is a short step to making jokes about students being dissected in the writing lab or tutors creating Frankenstein monsters. (37)

Carino's acknowledgment that the lab metaphor may be read pejoratively by some is certainly so—and will continue to be so for those who perceive *centers* as a better choice. Certainly the profession refers to these places as writing centers, but as two directors of writing *labs*, we as coauthors both also affirm how powerful local context is. For one of us (Harris), at Purdue University, a large state university, the term *center* has been co-opted, in part, by faculty-driven research centers. The university phone book lists twelve such centers. Many are research sites, a few offer health-related services, and most carry no indication of institutional centrality or of being student-oriented, helping places. Faculty with specialized research interests work in the Center for Applied Mathematics, the Center for Statistical Decision Sciences, the Center for New Crops and Plant Products, and so on; only those students who are ill go to the Urgent Care Center, and when stress overwhelms them, they head for the Psychological Services Center. Most students tend to see these latter two centers as places for the unhealthy or unstable, places to avoid if possible unless they are truly ill or having major emotional difficulties. As a result, they would prefer not to set foot in either center during their years on campus. But when they're working on class assignments, they regularly go for personal help to *help labs* for physics, math, biology, and so on. Each of these labs has a different name (e.g., Chemistry Resource Room, Math Tutorials), but in student lingo, they're all *labs*. The Writing Lab is thus one more "help place" in this context, particularly so when they are preparing résumés before job fairs or applying to professional schools or hoping to improve their GPAs by handing in better papers.

For the other of us (Fischer), at Clarke College, a small liberal arts college where everyone from students to faculty to maintenance workers to the college president refers to one another by first names, there are no *centers* except for the new Sports Center, which houses a pool, racquetball courts, basketball courts, and an indoor track. Although we've often joked about getting a NordicTrack and a rowing machine to help writers work through *block*, we feel no real similarity with that center. In an institution that has its roots in interactive learning and where *lecture hall* means fifty-five students in one class with one professor (an atrociously huge number on our campus), the word *center* seems somehow out of place. Our students also seek assistance in math labs, computer labs, and language labs. Ironically, our Writing Lab is located in the much-envied central-most place on campus in the new atrium building. But then again, perhaps this is not irony. Perhaps the centrality of our location grants us the privilege of maintaining our identity as a lab in a student-centered institution.

As coauthors of this essay we persist in calling our places *labs*; by so doing, we focus on the activity that (despite the vast differences in our two institutions with regard to clientele, size, and services) we see as core and kernel—namely, the one-to-one writing conference, an activity that is both intimate and experimental and that espouses that writing is best achieved through the trial and error of revision. Yet there exist strong voices in the writing-center community who prefer the term *center*. Some of them see the *lab/center* debate in terms of a growth and development metaphor—that their *labs* evolved into *centers*. Others prefer the term because of the connotation of centrality, and they view their use of the term *center* as a move to empowerment, not only viewing their work as central to writers but central to the institution through activities such as training teaching assistants, offering faculty workshops for writing-across-the-curriculum (WAC), and so on. If the institution responds to their vision, they are using the term appropriately. If there are political consequences because others challenge the use of *center*, then unpleasant turf battles can ensue. Like Carino (1992), who argues for the need to understand local context, Dave Healy (1995) invokes the metaphor of the writing center as church, a place where local conditions determine "particular styles, strategies, and missions based on many influences, the majority of which are more situational and demographic than ideological" (17).

In wondering if so many writing-center directors should have changed en masse from *lab* to *center*, Richard Leahy (1992) comments, "I can't help being a little disturbed by this belittling of *lab* and extolling of *center* as the better word when I consider how bland and meaningless the word *center* has become on so many college campuses" (43). He considers two forms of the word—centeredness and centrism. *Centeredness* suggests the best things a writing center can be with its connotations of purpose and community, but *centrism* suggests problems such as monopoly and self-importance. The danger of taking on too much, of becoming the center for all writing, is having to feel too responsible for everything going on in writing across the entire campus and curriculum. When Stephen North (1994) reconsidered his "idea" of a writing center, he too noted the need for retrenchment away from being the center of the institution, from the writing center's "taking upon its shoulders the whole institution's (real or imagined) sins of literacy" (17). But Carino also warns against the response of drawing inward, buying into the metaphor of the center as enclosed, thereby setting up a binary of we/they, opposing the center to the classroom. And an equally real danger, when insisting on the universal rightness of one term or another, can result in other problems. An unbending commitment to either *lab* or *center* as an eternal verity not to be questioned provokes the danger of conversations in which each writing center/lab faction talks past the other—unwilling either to budge from the stance being defended or unlikely to truly listen to the other's argument. That inflexible commitment suggests to those seeking advice about naming their new service that context is less important than the preference of a colleague in an institution far removed from the local setting of the new or reinvented place. Instead, decisions reached through institutional research—that close, analytical, and time-consuming study of one's own setting—are far more likely to have useful political impact because they result in knowing what fits that particular institution (Harris 1999).

The Shifting Sands of Metaphor

More recently, perhaps signaling a shift away from the *lab*/*center* debate, new names pregnant with new metaphors for writing centers are appearing on the scene. Terry Coye (1998) explains that at Gallaudet three separate programs—the Writing Center, the English Tutorial Center, and the English Literacy 2000 Program—were collapsed into a new, single unit that became English Works. "We like the name because 'works' can be either a verb or a noun, and can mean 'completed documents,' or 'factory,' or 'machinery,' or 'internal structure,' or 'labors,' or 'succeeds.' Take your pick! Since Gallaudet students are all deaf, the word also takes on meaning when translated into American Sign Language," Coye suggests. Similar attempts to identify writing centers in ways that more closely fit their work and their setting appear in names like the Writing Room, the Write Site, the Writery, the Write Place.

Perhaps it is this flexibility of metaphors and names that writing centers should seek most as they continue into future decades of writing-lab work. Ultimately, future metaphors should use the same criteria that tutors suggest to writers in the writing lab: audience, purpose, and rhetorical situations. To whom are those who reflect on the nature of writing centers and who name them actually talking? Who should be the audience for which metaphors? What do they hope to have result from their use of those metaphors? How will the given situations affect the use of those comparisons and result either in empowering or restricting writing centers?

When the audience is directors of writing centers, the metaphors that are applied serve to (a) reveal certain needs when writing-center people are seeking advice from each other; (b) reveal in what ways these centers are alike and unlike other colleagues' centers in order to advance discussions of practice and theory; and (c) let writing-center people cry on one another's shoulders. Metaphors are also hauled out to explain to colleagues new to the field of writing-center theory and practice how these glorious places function—as a way of making the unfamiliar familiar. Those who train tutors search for comparisons that enable tutors to see the multidimensional nature of their work; they are called tutors, consultants, counselors, writing assistants, midwives, mentors, partners, and coaches.

When the audience for metaphors for writing centers is other faculty who may promote or hinder the center's services among students, who may serve on committees that determine the director's tenure or promotion, or who may (or may not) avail themselves of the center's services, metaphors necessarily become more guarded. Although some of these colleagues do not hold the purse strings of the center's budget, they most certainly affect the continuance of these centers and labs in far-reaching ways. When they perceive those who direct the centers as hostile enemies in the turf wars over expertise, authority, or funding, new metaphors are needed to woo their understanding. Of course, metaphors claimed in dealing with this audience vary from institution to institution, depending on the attitude of the faculty as well as the kind of writing center. Across all campuses, concerns for how writing centers fit in or fail to fit in with composition programs, creative writing departments, WAC, and other writing programs arise in the metaphors that are applied. Those who present the center to its institutional public might call the people who work there collaborators, assistants, supporters, service providers, or corevisers, and the people who write the flyers, brochures, newspaper stories, reports, and announcements will highlight the ways in which the center complements or assists the work of classroom instructors and furthers the mission of the institution.

In ascending order of where metaphors may do the most harm or the most good, administrators are one of the trickiest audiences to inform and please. What metaphors help explain a center's work to them in terms of institutional mission? In terms of grants and other sources of funding? What images both appeal to marketing departments, retention committees, and admissions recruiters and yet satisfy the quest of those in writing centers to authentically represent themselves? Centers might be positioned as help places, student services that meet new institutional needs, high-tech writeries that match the institution's vision of its high-tech march to the twenty-first century, academic achievement labs—or even Mount Olympus when the struggle becomes really desperate. Writing-center directors might also heed the advice of one administrator who praised one of our writing labs as producing "a lot of bang for the buck," thereby turning a minimal budget into a cost-effective advantage, a quality no administrator scorns.

The most critical audience, perhaps, are the writers that centers and labs serve. With audiences that can include traditional-aged students, ESL students, working-class writers, nontraditional nighttime commuters, parents with children tagging along, community writers, and so on, providing metaphors that reveal the center's usefulness to these populations is challenging. Public representations might offer writing labs as craft studios where writers gather to weave together words or use metaphors that liken the lab or center to the local java joint where late-night discussions over thinking and writing occur and where occasionally a writer, struck by inspiration, will read poetry aloud while others offer advice. Like the social workers who offer support for those in need, writing centers can offer sympathetic ears as they help to retool those in need get through their difficulties of returning to academia, or they can be on-campus job-training services helping to get those résumés and letters of application in shape. Or they may become the fast food of writing services where they offer speedy service—students can have writing instruction their way—everything from French-fried grammar to hot-apple brainstorming and organizing-skills pie. With advice on documentation, brainstorming, and revision, centers can be sold as places where customers will find everything to satisfy their growling rhetorical hunger in one convenient place. If they can reach the "carryout" online writing labs (OWLs), they can do it from the comfort of their own desks. And, it might be implied, the advice will always please their palates.

With any of these audiences, as well as with those not named (elementary schoolchildren served through outreach programs, community business professionals taking writing workshops, groups of writers participating in readathons, and so on), the metaphors shift as do the purposes and the situations that envelop them. The metaphors that prove wise in the years when one's writing center is well funded and well staffed may prove foolish when a new administration with a new agenda threatens to disband the center altogether. The metaphors that inform students during final exam week when they seek assistance with take-home tests may utterly fail when it comes to seeking advice in revising submissions for a writing contest or preparing for writing proficiency exams or revising portfolios or writing in English as a foreign language.

Are writing centers, then, like a Möbius strip—a flexible bending ribbon that unexpectedly twists at the joining point so that both the inside and the outside lie along the same path? Like departments or programs on various campuses, aren't writing centers, too, ribbons where they are both among the mainstream and the revolutionaries resisting becoming too much a part of the university status quo? Through the center's services to writers, do they not also find themselves twisting in unexpected ways in order to meet changing needs and changing ways of writing? Or is this merely a contortionist view of writing-center work?

Like the associative linking behind writing centers' OWL web pages, are centers becoming more and more hypertextual in their advising clients, in training tutors, in networking with colleagues, in wooing both on- and off-campus funders, in offering liaison programs and workshops in the community, and in supporting or directing WAC programs so that even face-to-face labs operate in seeming haphazard order? Perhaps a more apt metaphor is the (World Wide) Web, where tutors act as button links connecting clients to their writing, to sources, to improvement, to their classroom teachers, and to the university itself. If this is the case, those who weave their writing centers into this web have to judge the losses when dealing in abbreviated time frames, lessened control of tutors, and sound bytes.

To complicate matters more, new advances in writing-center work require new metaphors. *Satellite center,* for example, finds astronaut tutors venturing outside the lab to attend to writing needs in dorms and student unions. Other emerging services will similarly beg for ways to explain the new and the unknown in known ways. In keeping with the belief that the metaphors that are applied need both to be flexible and to remain aware of local contexts, it is useful to listen to the following voices from WCenter, the electronic listserv for those in writing centers:

> OK, Sharon, let me get this straight. Writer/student is pilot? Tutor is navigator. Is the black box the director (sorry)? Is the air/water filled with the frequent turbulence of miscommunicated assignments, tunnel-visioned administrators, pedagogical dinosaurs (whoa, mixed metaphor). (Lerner 1994b)

> We envision our role as that of professional consultants. In many activities that require complex skills and demand practice, people take lessons from experts or hire professional Consultants. Individuals take golf lessons or cooking classes to become better golfers or more versatile cooks; businesses hire Consultants to improve their performance. The advice that experts provide for these purposes is not punitive, not judgmental, and not remedial, because it is sought after and valued. The Consultant views her client as a competent adult who is not an expert in her own field. (Kimball 1993)

> We have the "Waffle House" philosophy of service here. If we can't get to 'em, we holler, "Hey, welcome to the Writin' Center, have a seat, we'll be wit'cha in a second. A tutor goes by and offers coffee. Then we put down a menu, our sheet that asks what he/she wants that day.

We try to make sure the sheet is greasy and has coffee stains. . . . We ask that tables of two or more be reserved and we have lots of orange glass and music going. (Bagby 1998)

Hiking up in the Rockies with our five-year-old son, I was struck by how similar Andrew's hike was to our work in writing labs. As I watched him find his footings among jagged slopes and across hazardously slippery snow pockets, I tried to keep my own balance between letting him explore freely and cautioning him, "Pull back, you're getting too close to the edge." In writing centers it seems we do essentially this. (LaRue 1995)

Perhaps the writing center and its participants are more like a jazz combo. Tutors and students are all capable of creative, individual bursts, all work to bring each other to higher levels of performance, and all must work from a foundation in order to achieve coherence. Perhaps all tutors just have more developed chops, but in time the students will be there, too. (Lerner 1994a)

We could be as constant as clean, clear, drinkable water. Water takes the space of the vessel it's placed in much as a good writing advisor tries to fit with the writer's needs and the shape the writing is in. However, not all water is good water, so it's important to always make clear what one is doing and why. (Carbone 1998)

Carbone's call for the fluidity of water as metaphor for writing-center work is perhaps the best direction for future metaphors.

No metaphor can ground all that writing centers do or convey to all audiences in all contexts and situations who and what writing centers and labs are. I. A. Richards long ago identified an equation-like breakdown of metaphors in which the *vehicle* (gas station, hospital) carries or transfers meaning to the *tenor* (writing centers). When the tenor becomes common knowledge, the need for the metaphor is mitigated or nullified. Whereas many writing-center people saw themselves as marginalized in the early days, now there is as little reason to apply metaphors to writing centers as there is to apply them to campus libraries. Generally no one likens math or English departments, for example, to factories or gas stations or hospitals; rightly or wrongly, most people involved in the field of writing assume they know the work and roles of such departments. But not all writing labs are so firmly established within their institutions as to have such immediately recognizable identities, and even those that are may exist where some audiences and situations cry out for the use of metaphors.

One way to seek the Minotaur's way out of this maze is to return to the essential nature of metaphor and all figurative language. At the core, the comparison's power comes from the fact that the equation is literally *untrue*. Although the analogies that are used share similarities with the myriad ways writing-center people function within writing centers and resultantly in how they label tutors and directors, analogies must always break down at some point. It is at this breaking point that there appear the most significant ways out of the conundrums inherent in selecting such metaphors. Just as objects are defined by what they *are* as well as by what they *are not*, so, too, are writing labs defined by those breaks in the metaphorical comparisons that reveal what writing centers are not.

Tutors do not save the souls of papers; they do not imprison writers; they do not fill up the tanks of students' heads; they do not sell "good" or "correct" writing to customers (who could then return it); and they are not sweaty coaches trying to coax writers into beating the opposition at some competition. Those in writing centers know that, but are they also continually aware that they are really not coaches and consultants and midwives and pompom wavers—even though the terms are borrowed from such work? Do those who shape and direct their centers help all of their different audiences to understand where and how the metaphors break down? Through what centers are not and do not do, then, people in writing centers can see more clearly who and what they are. Constructing metaphors and then dissecting them to find their limitations is, finally, a useful exercise.

Thus, we coauthors of this essay issue an open invitation to join us in reflecting on the nature of writing centers and in continuing to assert new metaphors in the quest to illuminate more clearly a center's defining features and its position within the educational landscape. Together we can consider the hologram and how its images shift depending on the perspective from which it is viewed. We can also contemplate the destructive simplicity of the sound byte. Writing centers are more complex than images and metaphors can convey. Those of us in writing centers know this, but have we let all of our audiences know this too? And how do we do that, knowing full well that unarticulated perceptions caused by metaphors have a far longer shelf life than any new exploration that tries to wipe them out? Perhaps one way to contemplate this is to borrow that which Muriel Rukeyser claims of poetry. A writing center "is not its words or its images, any more than a symphony is its notes or a river its drops of water. It depends on the moving relations within itself . . . the work that it does is a transfer of human energy" (1996, xi).

Works Cited

Bagby, S. 1998. "Re: Appointments and Metaphors." Online posting. 12 October. In *WCENTER Archives* <http://www.ttu.edu/wcenter/9810/msg00136.html>.

Carbone, N. 1998. "'Constants' in Tutoring?" Online posting. 11 November. In *WCENTER Archives* <http://www.ttu.edu/wcenter/9811/msg00245.html>.

Carino, P. 1992. "What Do We Talk About When We Talk About Our Metaphors: A Cultural Critique of Clinic, Lab and Center." *The Writing Center Journal* 13 (1): 31–42.

Coye, T. 1998. "English Works!" E-mail to Katherine Fischer. 25 September.

Edlund, J. R. 1994. "Re: Burke/Liszt." Online posting. 25 July. In *WCENTER Archives* <http://www.ttu.edu/wcenter/9407/msg00384.html>.

Harris, M. 1999. "Diverse Research Methodologies at Work for Diverse Audiences: Shaping the Writing Center to the Institution." In *The Writing Program Administrator as Researcher*, edited by S. K. Rose and I. Weiser, 1–17. Portsmouth, NH: Boynton/Cook.

Healy, D. 1995. "In the Temple of the Familiar: The Writing Center as Church." In *Writing Center Perspectives,* edited by B. L. Stay, C. Murphy, and E. H. Hobson, 12–25. Emmitsburg, MD: NWCA.

Hobson, E. 1994. "Writing Center Practice Often Counters Its Theory. So What?" In *Intersections: Theory-Practice in the Writing Center*, edited by J. A. Mullin and R. Wallace, 1–10. Urbana, IL: NCTE.

Kimball, S. 1993. The Undergraduate Writing Center, UT Staff Handbook. University of Texas at Austin.

Krapohl, C. 1989. "Late Night at the Writing Center: Service Station or Oasis?" *Writing Lab Newsletter* 14 (2): 9.

LaRue, L. 1995. [Katherine Fischer]. "It's All Done with Mirrors!" Online posting. 6 December. In *WCENTER Archives* <http://www.ttu.edu/wcenter/9512/msg00178.html>.

Leahy, R. 1992. "Of Writing Centers, Centeredness, and Centrism." *The Writing Center Journal* 13 (1): 43–52.

Lerner, N. 1994a. "Re: Tutors and Orchestras." Online posting. 19 July. In *WCENTER Archives* <http://www.ttu.edu/wcenter/9407/msg00256.html>.

———. 1994b. "Re: Writing Center Metaphor." Online posting. 4 August. In *WCENTER Archives* <http://www.ttu.edu/wcenter/9408/msg00015.html>.

Lunsford, A. 1991. "Collaboration, Control, and the Idea of a Writing Center." *The Writing Center Journal* 12 (1): 3–10.

Murphy, C. 1994. "The Writing Center and Social Constructionist Theory." In *Intersections: Theory-Practice in the Writing Center*, edited by J. A. Mullin and R. Wallace, 25–38. Urbana, IL: NCTE.

North, S. 1994. "Revisiting 'The Idea of a Writing Center.'" *The Writing Center Journal* 15 (1): 7–19.

Pemberton, M. A. 1992. "The Prison, the Hospital, and the Madhouse: Redefining Metaphors for the Writing Center." *Writing Lab Newsletter* 17 (1): 11–16.

Purcell, K. C. 1998. "Making Sense of the Meaning: ESL and the Writing Center." *Writing Lab Newsletter* 22 (6): 1–5.

Rabuck, D. F. 1995. "Giving Birth to Voice: The Professional Writing Tutor as Midwife." In *Writing Center Perspectives*, edited by B. L. Stay, C. Murphy, and E. H. Hobson, 112–19. Emmitsburg, MD: NWCA.

Rukeyser, M. 1996. *The Life of Poetry*. Ashfield, MA: Paris Press.

Severino, C. 1994. "Writing Centers as Linguistic Contact Zones and Borderlands." *Writing Lab Newsletter* 19 (4): 1–5.

Sontag, S. 1978. *Illness as Metaphor*. New York: Farrar, Straus & Giroux.

4

Peer Tutoring

Keeping the Contradiction Productive

Jane Cogie

> At times I felt as confused as Janelle [the tutee] . . . because
> I'm trying to absorb this information, and it's kind of like
> dancing . . . quickly . . . trying to think of routes and direc-
> tions we can take. (Ken, a graduate assistant tutor, in response
> to watching a videotape of one of his tutoring sessions)

Ken's analogy here between his tutoring session and improvised dancing captures the tensions inherent in collaborative writing-center work,
even for seasoned tutors. The most apparent tension is the speed with
which decisions must be made to move sessions forward meaningfully.
Yet embedded in the pressure for meaningful momentum is the tension
of attending to the conflicting roles of a peer tutor: peer versus tutor
(Trimbur 1987), supporter of the student versus representative of the
university, advocate of the writing process versus expert on the written
product. Peer tutors are given few answers on how to balance these
roles with sensitivity to the accompanying political and pedagogical
issues. Added to these pressures may be student expectations for proofreading by an expert and the fear of inadequacy that often underpins
those expectations. At work, as well, is the potential impact of the
tutor's and student's age, gender, and educational level. The ways the
tutor and student deal with all of these factors help determine the location of power and the nature of learning in their collaborative dance.

The pressure for Ken in his session with Janelle likely stemmed at
least in part from his concern that, after six semesters of tutoring, he
found it difficult to tell if he was intervening too much, a concern he

had mentioned during an earlier training workshop. To explore his role as tutor and its effect on the student-tutor relationship, he and I decided to tape one of his sessions with Janelle, his least confident tutee, for both his benefit as tutor and mine as coordinator of tutor training.

Agreeing with Andrea Lunsford (1991) that writing centers "need to be well versed in a variety of types of collaboration including hierarchical and dialogic" (7), I felt it important to complicate views of the tutor's role in recent training workshops. We discussed articles that disrupt a simplifying opposition of nondirective and directive tutoring. We looked, for instance, at Marilyn Cooper's article (1994) that focuses on tutors helping students gain the agency to balance university demands with their own agendas, and Lad Tobin's chapter (1993, 40–56) that challenges teachers not to smooth over the tension in one-on-one conferences but to use it productively. Yet in our role-playing activities, the polarization of the extremes crept back in. Role-plays of restrained tutor power left space for student discovery of power, whereas role-plays of direct tutor power enforced student powerlessness.

I let these exaggerated models reappear, I think, because it felt dangerous to conclude training without providing touchstones to ward off tutor dominance that can easily result from directive tutoring, and to foster student engagement more demonstrably at work in nondirective tutoring. Alice Gillam, Susan Callaway, and Katherine Wikoff (1994) discuss the confusing message tutors are sent in their training. Tutors are asked on the one hand to restrain their authority so as to focus on the student while on the other to assert it so as to aid student understanding. As a result of that message, "tutors frequently evaluate their tutoring effectiveness in terms of their use of authority" (166).

Perhaps the best way to combat a stereotyped view of the location of power in one-on-one work is by analyzing how power functions in actual sessions. In this chapter, then, I will explore writing-center practice and its tension with the stereotypes of the directive and nondirective tutoring modes, first as discussed in recent writing-center scholarship and then as played out in the videotaped session of Ken and Janelle.

Beyond Directive Versus Nondirective Tutoring

It is not surprising that directive tutoring continues to be perceived as questionable. Sessions in which tutors talk more than students and provide them with wording appear not only hierarchical and concerned with product rather than process, but also politically and pedagogically regressive, limiting the student's agency and participation in knowledge construction. Compounding the distrust of directive tutoring is the ease with which it can be used by tutors who doubt they have the time or the finesse to negotiate problems with the student's writing process. Indeed, far more students and tutors have internalized the directive dynamic than the nondirective one (Gillam, Callaway, and Wikoff 1994, 162). Directive tutoring, then, may result more from taking the path of least resistance than from a genuine response to the needs of students.

Such unintentional domination seems to occur in a session, analyzed by Carol Severino (1992), between Henry, a master's degree tutor, and Joe, an African American Army veteran and first-year college student. Fear that without timely assistance Joe will lose control of his paper appears to draw Henry to these leading questions: "Now, is your attitude shaped let's say toward the white race, for example? Is that what [your paper is] going to center on?" (57). Perhaps because of a lack of confidence in Joe's ability, Henry preempts Joe's opportunity to engage in the process of narrowing his topic. As Severino notes, the directive approach Henry falls into may well benefit "the efficiency of producing a product" yet does so at the expense of "the play of process" (62). This session surely falls into the stereotype of the directive session that is unproductive both pedagogically and politically.

While much directive tutoring is to be avoided, it is far from monolithic, the tutor uniformly asserting authority at the expense of the student's authority and valuing product at the expense of process. Activities that on the surface may seem too directive may indeed provide the support the student needs to advance as a writer. The pedagogical importance of such support is affirmed in Annemarie Palinscar's study of novice writers in one-on-one sessions (1986). The tutor's role in helping the study's subjects acquire cognitive strategies involved not simply "getting the students to talk" but clear guidance that allowed them to reach beyond their independent learning level (96). Her findings, as Palinscar notes (74), parallel those in Lev Vygotsky's studies (1978) showing that children with adult guidance learn beyond their own independent problem-solving ability (84–91).

In making decisions about guidance, however, one must consider the soundness not just of the pedagogy but also of the politics the pedagogy reflects. The interconnectedness of politics and pedagogy is highlighted in Sarah Freedman and Melanie Sperling's study (1985) of a teacher's responses to groups of higher-achieving and lower-achieving students. The study found that the teacher withheld from the lower-achieving students productive criticism and insider knowledge needed for academic success, the sort of advice she freely offered the higher-achieving students (125, 128). Laurel Johnson Black (1998) discovered a similar privileging of one group over another in her conferences with classroom students. However, her case involved privileging students already initiated in disciplinary discourse over those remaining uninitiated. In reviewing the conference transcripts, she found that, without knowing it, she had used disciplinary language with students who themselves used this language and withheld it from those who did not (30).

The teacher's behavior with the deprived groups in both studies may be explained in part by the tendency, noted by Black, for a speaker in conversation "to match" the other speaker's use of language so as to "equalize" the status of the two (30). Yet there is obvious irony in this behavior since, through such equalization, lower-achieving individuals may never gain the situated knowledge needed for academic success. There is, then, more than one way for a tutor to dominate a student. The decision to remain consistently more peer than tutor and avoid what may seem a teacherly sharing of information may not be the best way to empower a student.

Just as directive tutoring may at times be student centered, so nondirective tutoring when purely interpreted may be tutor centered, as appeared to happen in Morgan's nondirective session with Fanny, recounted by Anne DiPardo (1992). Despite model restraint in efforts to draw out Fanny, a Native American student raised on a reservation, Morgan, her middle-class, African American tutor, failed to listen for the cultural context of Fanny's ideas and her conflict in articulating those ideas within the academic context (131–32). Thus she failed to help Fanny negotiate this conflict and move forward with her essays.

Listening effectively may involve other kinds of sensitivity, such as the recognition that for some students nondirectiveness can translate into a covert kind of directiveness. If students sense an undeclared agenda, they can feel manipulated, as Dina Fayer (1994) reports her male ex-Marine tutee feeling when she follows the minimalist approach of her training (13). Because of this student's top-down learning paradigm, Fayer's minimalist attempts at equalizing their roles became for him, and consequently for her, a mere "rhetoric of equality," to use Jane Melnick's words (1984), a means of trying to deny the "inevitability" of the tutor's authority to determine the basic approach of a session (17).

It was out of my interest in further understanding the political tensions within the student-tutor relationship and Ken's desire to reflect on his own use of tutor authority that I arranged the videotape project between Ken, a white Ph.D. student in literature, and Janelle, a white, traditional-aged, first-year student and one of his regular weekly appointments. The project included my viewing and discussing their fifty-minute video with each of them separately. Janelle was, at the time of the session, an inexperienced and unconfident writer, enrolled in English Composition 102. She had met with Ken eight times before this session. The agenda for the conference originated in Janelle's concern over her instructor's comment that her research paper needed to focus less on her own vegetarianism and more on vegetarianism in general.

The Location of Power in Ken and Janelle's Collaborative Dance

Any analysis of this conference, especially one focusing on the location of power, would need to consider Janelle's increasing level of involvement despite Ken's talking considerably more than she, 70 percent to her 30 percent. At the session's outset, in response to Ken's question, "Do you have an idea where you're going with the paper right now?" Janelle replies, "I don't know. I'm kinda stuck." Near the end of the session, in response to Ken's saying, "The only advice I would give is for you to keep thinking the way you have been," she concludes, "Yeah. I'm not stuck anymore." This change, and her ability several lines later to sum up clearly her plans for revision, suggests the session's overall productivity. However, if one were to judge solely by the amount of talking done by each collaborator, the session would be labeled hierarchical and likely to contribute to Janelle's written product but not to her growth as a writer.

Indeed, some strategies that Ken uses, though not as extreme as Henry's with Joe, would likely be labeled as hierarchical. In several sections, he leads Janelle toward solutions before testing to see if she needs assistance, and in other sections, he gives her terms that sum up her perspective or asks leading questions. There are a total of three leading questions and eleven closed questions overall, though nine of the closed questions are to confirm a point or to solicit information. There are also, however, student-centered strategies. Ken lets Janelle's concerns set the agenda and asks thirteen open-ended questions. Also, four times, Ken reads aloud passages from her draft and twice asks her to write down her ideas. Perhaps most important, he leaves plenty of wait time for her to respond to his questions. Still other tactics, such as summaries of her points, validation of her draft, and expository comments on aspects of writing, fall somewhere between these extremes. Although not directing Janelle to specific solutions, these activities, labeled "metacommunicative" and "teacher talk" by Michael Stubbs, reflect an expert-novice relationship (1983, 51–53).

To understand the politics of this session, however, it is important not simply to categorize Ken's strategies but also to analyze the range of power issues they reflect. Before turning to the politics in particular portions of the session, I will consider possible reasons for Ken's overall dominance in the number of words spoken. One likely factor is the degree to which hierarchical teaching is ingrained in our culture and

becomes particularly difficult to combat when the age and educational
level of tutor and student differ significantly, as they do with Janelle
and Ken. Added to the pressure of this top-down learning model is the
likely impact of gender issues. In studying conferencing between
classroom teachers and students, Black (1998) found that although
female students talked more with male than with female instructors,
24.3 percent of the total talk as compared to 13.6 percent, they asked
male teachers more questions and were "more tentative about their
knowledge" with them, frequently using the phrase "I don't know"
(64). Following this pattern, Janelle asks eight questions of Ken during
the conference, six of which look to him for judgment. She also replies
"I don't know" twice to Ken's questions. However, she breaks with
this pattern, twice reflecting doubt about Ken's suggestions, and Ken
himself adds an "I don't know [myself]" to two of his questions. Overall, though, Janelle seems either to go along or to be comfortable with
Ken's taking the lead. Indeed, in our interview, her comment, "I always
get stuck, and as soon as I go to him, I get ideas" seems to confirm this
pattern of her as follower, although her emphasis on "I get ideas"
seems to suggest that in the process of his leading her, she herself gains
authority.

The power issue more specific to this particular session stems from
Janelle's lack of situated knowledge of academic research and the role
personal perspectives can play within it. Ken must deal with this lack
of knowledge in relation not only to his own greater knowledge but
also to the differences between his views of research and her instructor's. An early section in the conference that reveals this complicated
dynamic occurs shortly after Janelle responds to Ken's interest in her
topic: "I don't know if I need more research or if it's good to have my
personal experience in it or what," and then asserts she is "stuck."
Shortly after that, Ken finishes reading her draft:

Ken: I really did enjoy this draft, and one of the first questions you
    asked me was you thought maybe it was too personal . . . and that
    was your concern . . . is mixing personal and the research. Now
    given [your instructor] has said, his comments have said, try to be
    less personal and more concerned with vegetarianism in general.
    Now did he elaborate on this in any way?

Janelle: No.

Ken: No. Okay. Because now while . . . I mean, it seems to me start-
    ing off from a personal basis makes a lot of sense, because, I mean,
    you are a vegetarian, so what better place to start than something
    you personally are involved in, but he is concerned about the fact
    that we have to be careful about the personal angle, so we have to

find a way to work in this switch. One way we might do this . . . I
was thinking about the introduction to the paper, basically the first
two paragraphs of the paper kind of set out what you're going to
do, um, in fact, do you mind if I read the first paragraph?

Janelle: No.

Ken: Okay. Let's read the first paragraph. I want to think about maybe
. . . we're thinking about where the paper is going, you need to
make eight pages, you're halfway there, you've incorporated
research . . . right now I want to think about where . . . how the
paper is focused in the initial stages of the paper . . . um. (Ken
reads Janelle's introduction aloud.) Okay . . . so that's the first
paragraph we have. Now give . . . if we're just reading the first
paragraph and we're thinking about where the entire paper is going
as a research paper, where is it going based on this first paragraph?

Janelle: Probably the effects of eating meat and what it does to you.

Ken handles his authority on research and the role of personal
experience within it with care. For instance, in his first segment quoted
above, he uses his authority to leave space for Janelle's concern. As he
words it, "Your concern . . . is mixing the personal and the research"—
letting it remain separate from the instructor's—" . . . his comments
have said try to be less personal and more concerned with vegetarianism in general." Ken may be particularly sensitive to her concern
because he sees the limits that following the instructor's demand
would place on her agency in this essay. As he told me in our interview,
"Had I been evaluating the paper myself as her instructor, I probably
wouldn't have said it was too personal. . . . I probably wouldn't have
made that simple statement."

The complexity of Ken's role in having to deal with both Janelle's
and her instructor's doubts about including the personal becomes clear
in his second segment quoted above, where he emphasizes the value of
the personal in her introduction: "Because now while . . . I mean, it
seems to me starting off from a personal basis makes a lot of sense,
because, I mean, you are a vegetarian, so what better place to start than
something you personally are involved in, but he is concerned about
the fact that we have to be careful about the personal angle, so we have
to find a way to work in this switch." This passage seems noticeably
effortful, with the slowing force of the two *becauses* and the two *I
mean*s registering the pressure of supporting her position in the face of
the instructor's misguided stance. Indeed, this careful affirmation of
Janelle's personal stance, distancing the instructor's position—"so we
have to find a way to work in this switch"—without alienating her
from it, seems an example of the "cogent critiques of assignments"

that, as Marilyn Cooper (1994) notes, "often leak out in writing center sessions even when [the tutors] don't make them explicit" (140). It indicates as well the sense in which Ken, though himself in a position of power relative to Janelle, must struggle with institutional standards different from his own.

It is worth noting that Ken's *I mean*s in this last section differ in audience from those used in conferences of classroom teachers studied by Black (1998). In discussing her subjects' use of this phrase as a discourse marker, "[positioning] a speaker in relation to the information or another speaker" (42), she notes that her classroom teachers employ this phrase with students to "acknowledge the lack of shared knowledge" (47). The acknowledgment in Ken's *I mean*s seems as much directed to Janelle's instructor, his equal in the academic hierarchy, as to Janelle. His frequent use of a second term, *okay,* noticeable as well in the section quoted above (he uses it a total of sixty-two times in the session in comparison to *I mean,* used thirteen times), is worth noting; its nonevaluative form of affirmation at once confirms his role as manager and serves to soften its hierarchical impact.

The tension in Ken's restraining his role as manager is evident in his attempt to bridge Janelle's and her instructor's concerns at the end of his second segment in the above quoted section: "One way we might do this . . . I was thinking about the introduction to the paper, basically the first two paragraphs of the paper kind of set out what you're going to do, um . . . in fact, do you mind if I read the first paragraph?" In "One way we might do this . . . ," he begins to assert a solution but quickly pulls back, perhaps listening to his minimalist conscience or remembering the need to encourage Janelle's authority. In any case, he swerves to a distinctly nondirective technique, reading aloud a portion of Janelle's text. After reading the paragraph, he concludes with a question that again reveals the tension of withholding knowledge so as to involve Janelle and live up to the peer aspect of their relationship: "Now, if we're just reading the first paragraph and we're thinking about where the entire paper is going as a research paper, where is it going based on the first paragraph?" Clearly, this question has an agenda, to help Janelle discover the need to integrate her general research focus into her personally oriented introduction. However, she misses his hint. While Ken's attempt fails and he must tackle this problem again later, Janelle, in her reply concerning her focus, makes her first active response to her essay, "[probably] the effects of eating meat and what it does to you."

This small breakthrough is followed by other small but more crucial ones, breakthroughs in which Janelle sets forth her essay's purpose and audience and hits upon the idea of using interviews with vegetarian friends as research. Yet this first breakthrough and others early on are hard won, gained through a range of strategies that carry for Ken the tension of balancing student and tutor authority. Would Ken, in facing the problem with her introduction, have served himself and Janelle better both politically—by revealing his authority more openly—and pedagogically—by greater clarity of advice—had he simply explained the problem to her? In exploring rhetorical strategies in tutor-client conversations, Susan Blau, John Hall, and Tracy Strauss (1998) conclude that they saw "too many examples of tutors dancing around a direct question, when they clearly knew the answer, wasting the already too-short time they had to spend with their clients. Generally speaking, a directive approach seems better suited for content, nondirective for process" (38). In Ken and Janelle's session, an outright explanation might have increased the efficiency and political openness, yet Janelle's gain in beginning to focus her revision might have been lost.

Ken's lengthy response below to Janelle's first breakthrough is another instance where one might question whether straightforward directiveness might have proved more effective. After his initial affirmation, "Okay. That's good," the connection he intends to make with Janelle's statement of her focus is not clear-cut:

Ken: Okay. That's good. Now . . . and if there's anywhere in the paper, I mean, obviously, when the personal material is coming out, it is in the first paragraph. Now in the rest of the paper as it develops, you go in and you talk about the different types, you describe the different types of vegetarians, which I think is very nicely done and very necessary to this paper. People are often concerned about, you know, everyone lumps vegetarians into one category, a vegetarian is this, and you seem to nicely describe that, no, not all vegetarians are alike and, in fact, at one point you say, you know, some people call themselves vegetarians and they start eating fish, chicken, and eggs. You correctly point out here that you don't think they should be called vegetarians.

One begins to see that Ken's review of Janelle's paper has more than one purpose. It reconnects with Janelle's question about personal experience but also provides a more complete answer than did Janelle to his own earlier question on her paper's direction. His answer, outlining the split between the first paragraph's "obviously . . . personal material" and the rest of the paper's focus on "different types of vegetarians," would allow her to see this organizational problem if she were ready. Yet perhaps most important for Janelle, his description affirms the real substance of the research portion of her essay, about which she has so little confidence. In its length and undeclared agendas, this sum-

mary could be said to hover near Lunsford's "collaboration in which
the same old authoritarian control masquerades as democracy" (1991,
7). But in its confidence-building affirmation of her research and the
unheralded modeling of a more complete summary, it seems more like
a version of the hierarchical collaboration Lunsford asserts writing
centers need to be ready to employ (7).

Evidence of Janelle's growing confidence increases after they
again discuss her instructor's demands. After Janelle reconfirms that
the instructor's only emphasis is the need to be less personal, she inter-
rupts Ken's "Okay. Let's . . . ," with the statement, "I think it would be
boring if I left it all research." Ken's response below reveals the extent
to which for Janelle, at least in the context of their relationship, this is
a somewhat startling, assertive thing to say:

Ken: If you . . . oh, you mean if you took the personal out? Oh, I think
you're right. Yeah. And I think your feelings about that are important because research papers are supposed to be interesting . . .
that's not why we write them. The task then becomes how . . . do
I write about something that I have personal investment in, in a
kind of research-oriented fashion. And I guess now I could ask you
a tough question . . . realizing you're not fully through the process
yet, what is. . . . what do you think the purpose of the paper is at
this point?

The degree of Ken's surprise here at her assertion registers in his
false start, "If you . . . ," followed by the two *oh*s, which Deborah
Schiffrin (1987) notes in her discussion of *oh* as a discourse marker "is
more likely to be used when locally provided information does not cor-
respond to a speaker's prior expectations" (90–91).

Perhaps in part because of her new assertiveness, Ken himself
becomes less tentative and puts to her a genuinely open-ended question, quoted above, on her purpose: "What do you think the purpose of
the paper is at this point?" In her rough reply, "Make people more . . .
Vegetarianism . . . Realize like what a vegetarian is, how they're different, not every vegetarian is the same, does the same thing," she
shows herself willing to risk tentativeness to formulate her ideas. Ken,
again impressed, responds, "Okay. Actually, write some of those ideas
down right now. . . . Those are good ideas." A few lines later, in
response to a question from Ken on whether her essay is informative
or persuasive, she replies, "Well, actually, I guess what I've written so
far is more persuasive, but I'd like it to be more informative. I don't
want to push somebody to be a vegetarian. I just want them to realize
what a vegetarian is." When she goes on to say, "I think people sort of
look down on vegetarians. . . . We're no different from them. We just

don't eat meat," Ken then sums up the idea implicit in her focus as "trying to get rid of a stereotype of what a vegetarian is." While she ends up using his term *stereotype* in her revision and cites it in our interview as the most useful aspect of the session, she does not mention it here but moves on to ask, "Is that considered research if you interview like a friend or someone who is a vegetarian?" After he affirms the validity of interviews as research and then reads aloud the next paragraph, Janelle says without prompting, "I can totally expand on that now that I'm reading it . . . ," a move that reflects her strengthened role in the collaboration.

The session's concluding moments narrated here indicate the evolution of Ken and Janelle's interaction from guide and guided to a more equal interchange in which both of them move the session forward. The authority she takes away from this session is evident in her revised draft, where she places herself more clearly within the spectrum of vegetarians and includes new material from interviews with friends, thus not only preserving her personal focus but more fully integrating it with the research aspect of her essay. Janelle initiates both these changes while Ken validates and helps focus the points from the original draft that her changes build on.

In reflecting on this session, one might ask if Janelle might have become empowered sooner had Ken been less hierarchical and more purely nondirective in his approach, asking more open-ended questions earlier. Certainly, that is possible. Yet, as noted earlier, one might also reasonably ask if Janelle might have become more empowered sooner had Ken been more directive, explicitly diagnosing problems. Certainly, that is possible too. The point here is that, given the dual need for guidance and discovery in most students, any strategy involves risk. Fostering student authority is not a matter of following a single approach and avoiding another. The authority of students may grow from moves as diverse as asking them tough questions, providing summaries or terms to help them conceptualize points and build confidence, and helping them negotiate assignment demands, gain the necessary situated knowledge, or try out aspects of the writing process. Ken's mixed approach provides an example of the potential of combining such diverse strategies. Although his approach is in no way the inevitable one to use, it succeeds in helping Janelle gain more confidence and make discoveries that feed into a productive revision.

Complicating the pure opposition between directive and nondirective tutoring—what Gillam, Callaway, and Wikoff (1994) call the confusing "either/or" view of tutor authority (195)—to make room for greater flexibility does not free tutors from the tension of monitoring the effects of their authority on the student. The right balance of guidance by the tutor and exploration by the student is rarely clear-cut. Added to the tension of this balancing act is the need to be wary of inequities between the collaborators—differences in academic status, availability of situated knowledge, the predisposition to hierarchical learning, as well as issues of gender and age—that can shape the learning accessible to students. Yet countering the polarization of directive and nondirective tutoring can perhaps help tutors become more willing to risk a variety of strategies with the awareness that authority expressed by tutors, a given in any approach, need not preclude the students' discovery of powers of their own.

Works Cited

Black, L. J. 1998. *Between Talk and Teaching: Reconsidering the Writing Conference*. Logan, UT: Utah State University Press.

Blau, S., J. Hall, and T. Strauss. 1998. "Exploring the Tutor/Client Conversation: A Linguistic Analysis." *The Writing Center Journal* 19 (1): 19–48.

Cooper, M. M. 1994. "Really Useful Knowledge: A Cultural Agenda for Writing Centers." *The Writing Center Journal* 14 (2): 97–111.

DiPardo, A. 1992. "'Whispers of Coming and Going': Lessons from Fannie." *The Writing Center Journal* 12 (2): 125–44.

Fayer, D. 1994. "Tutors' Column: Orthodoxy and Effectiveness." *Writing Lab Newsletter* 18 (5): 13.

Freedman, S. W., and M. Sperling. 1985. "Written Language Acquisition: The Role of Response and the Writing Conference." In *The Acquisition of Written Language: Response and Revision*, edited by S. W. Freedman, 106–30. Norwood, NJ: Ablex.

Gillam, A., S. Callaway, and K. H. Wikoff. 1994. "The Role of Authority and the Authority of Roles in Peer Writing Tutorials." *Journal of Teaching Writing* 12 (2): 161–98.

Lunsford, A. 1991. "Collaboration, Control, and the Idea of a Writing Center." *The Writing Center Journal* 12 (1): 3–10.

Melnick, J. F. 1984. "The Politics of Writing Conferences: Describing Authority Through the Speech Act Theory." *The Writing Center Journal* 4 (2): 9–21.

Palinscar, A. S. 1986. "The Role of Dialogue in Providing Scaffolded Instruction." *Educational Psychologist* 21 (1/2): 73–98.

Schiffrin, D. 1987. *Discourse Markers*. Cambridge: Cambridge University Press.

Severino, C. 1992. "Rhetorically Analyzing Collaboration(s)." *The Writing Center Journal* 13 (1): 53–64.

Stubbs, M. 1983. *Discourse Analysis: The Sociolinguistic Analysis of Natural Language*. Chicago: University of Chicago Press.

Tobin, L. 1993. *Writing Relationships: What Really Happens in the Composition Class*. Portsmouth, NH: Boynton/Cook.

Trimbur, J. 1987. "Peer Tutoring: A Contradiction in Terms?" *The Writing Center Journal* 7 (2): 21–28.

Vygotsky, L. S. 1978. *Mind in Society: The Development of Higher Psychological Processes*. Cambridge, MA: Harvard University Press.

5

Graduate Students in the Writing Center

Confronting the Cult of (Non)Expertise

Carrie Shively Leverenz

Four years ago, when I was a relatively new writing-center director, I received a phone call from a woman I'll call Marguerite. Marguerite began by telling me that she was a returning student, in her forties, who had a busy schedule and did not have time to waste. She had been a painter before she decided to get a master's degree in art history, mostly because her partner had left her and she needed to be able to get a job to support her young daughter. Her professors had told her she needed to work on her writing, and having been out of academe for so long, she thought they must be right. She preferred working with a woman, someone experienced in tutoring graduate students who might also be interested in her ideas, which included Jungian psychoanalysis, African tribalism, and herbal drawings. Because she would be paying for her writing-center credits out of her student loan money herself (my center offers primarily for-credit appointments), and because she was already quite a bit in debt, she needed to know: Could we help her? Would it be worth her time and money?

I open with this scenario because it brings to the forefront the political nature of writing-center work as it intersects with students' acquisition of disciplinary expertise. What complications occur when writing centers intervene in a process thought to be the purview of disciplinary experts or, at the very least, a process that graduate students are expected to manage on their own?

When graduate students come to the writing center, everyone's expertise is at stake: the graduate student's expertise in a particular discipline, the tutor's expertise in writing and tutoring, and the disciplinary professor's expertise as a teacher-mentor. Most who have invested time, energy, and money in earning advanced degrees think of their expertise as a crucial part of their professional identity. Moreover, as Nancy Grimm points out in "Rearticulating the Work of the Writing Center" (1996), identity is "inevitably relational." What makes writing-center work political, according to Grimm, is having to manage "the inevitable tensions or hostilities in those relations" (527). When a student like Marguerite approaches the writing center for help, our mission statement, which proclaims that we work with any writer on any kind of writing at any point in the writing process, leads us to embrace her with open arms. But given the tensions and hostilities that can emerge when professional identities are threatened or transgressed, we ought to take seriously her question. What kind of expertise do we have to offer Marguerite, and will our help be worth her time and money?

In an attempt to answer this question, I conducted a yearlong study of the graduate students who came to the writing center I direct. Eighteen students completed surveys that asked how they found out about our services, what their expectations were, and whether we had met their expectations. I observed tutorials of eight graduate students enrolled for credit, and I collected writing samples from four of the graduate students I observed. I also interviewed the ten tutors who worked with graduate-student writers during this period and three of the graduate students being tutored. A few of the graduate students I studied were seeking help with writing they were doing in their first graduate classes, classes they were taking in the hopes of being formally admitted to a graduate program. One woman was required to enroll in the writing center before being admitted to a graduate program in the College of Human Science. Several were quite gifted international students who were referred to us either through their programs or through the International Student Center. Others, like Marguerite, were returning graduate students who needed help understanding what was being asked of them. All wished to improve their writing in order to increase their success in their field. Although the purpose of my research was to find out more about the graduate students who came to my writing center, I believe the political tensions that I saw emerging around the question of professional expertise are likely to occur in other academic institutions as well.

Like many of the undergraduate students who come to the writing center, these graduate-student writers typically say they need help with editing and grammar. As with undergraduate writers, the tutors who work with graduate students often feel conflicted about when and how to work on grammar when these writers also need help with more global and rhetorical issues. Graduate students who are told they need to work on their grammar may very well perceive this work as a required part of entry into their profession and may be frustrated by a tutor's attempt to talk about anything else. The tutors themselves are more likely to second-guess their ability—and their responsibility—to deal with content issues when they are unfamiliar with both the students' specialized subjects and their discipline-based genres. One graduate student, Lori, brought to her tutorials papers on which her professor had marked only her grammatical errors. Her tutor, on the other hand, was more concerned that Lori seemed to have difficulty explaining the theories she was referring to in her writing. The tutor admitted feeling conflicted about focusing on grammar when she thought Lori might benefit from more attention to her content. But was it the tutor's place to question the content when the student's professor did not? In another example of the quest for grammar expertise, a graduate student who had been coming to the writing center for several semesters stopped by with a grant proposal that needed to be mailed that day. She had already worked on it with a tutor earlier in the week and just wanted a final proofreading, which I reluctantly agreed to do. Later, this student stopped me in the hall to exclaim over the help I had given her. When I told her that any of the tutors could have done what I did, she insisted that they were not as competent, pointing out that even her major professor who was an editor no longer caught all of her errors. For her, I was the true expert, and access to my expertise increased the chance that her grant proposal would be funded, thus improving her success as a professional.

I won't rehearse here all the reasons why writing centers resist being identified with having expertise in grammar. Suffice it to say that writing centers do not want to be seen as experts *only* in grammar. And yet, is it unreasonable for graduate students and their supervising professors to look to the writing center for help with grammar? Perhaps writing centers are seen as sites of grammar expertise because of the perceived need to assign every kind of knowledge to some disciplinary box and to think of educational units as boxes with specialized knowledge inside. Cheryl Geisler, in her book *Academic Literacy and the Nature of Expertise* (1994), defines expertise as "a claim to the command of an arcane knowledge that goes beyond everyday understanding" (53). What could be more arcane than English grammar?

But if writing centers aren't sites of expertise in grammar, or *only* grammar, what kind of expertise can students like Marguerite hope to find? Although many writing centers develop expertise in writing across the curriculum or ESL, for example, these kinds of local expertise are not necessarily part of what all writing centers do. Nevertheless, most writing centers do share a core of beliefs and practices that inform most of their mission statements and that might be said to constitute writing-center expertise. By now it is practically a cliché to repeat the idea of a writing center so eloquently articulated by Stephen North in his 1984 *College English* essay. Although North himself later revised his idea of a writing center, the characteristics of writing-center practice that he espoused in the earlier article—student centered, process oriented, focused on writers not texts, based on conversation—is probably the best-known articulation of the writing-center community's disciplinary values. In "Talking in the Middle: Why Writers Need Writing Tutors," an essay that appeared in *College English* more than ten years later, Muriel Harris (1995) describes writing-center work in almost identical terms. Relying heavily on student responses to tutorials, Harris argues that what's valuable about writing centers is that through conversation, tutors get writers involved in generating ideas about writing, help to increase writers' self-confidence, and help to translate and interpret academic language and academic culture.

If the characteristics of expertise put forth by Geisler (1994) are considered, it is easy to see why writing-center expertise is difficult to describe. In an extensive study that compared the way that novices and experts solve problems, Geisler found that in addition to knowing more about their subject, experts also "represent the world—or the part of it that lies within their expertise—in a way more abstract and less literal than laypersons" (64). In addition, experts use elaborate reasoning procedures that Geisler argues may grow out of a "need for experts to convince others—often nonexperts—to accept and act upon their expert judgments" (65). And experts are better than novices at knowing how to take into account case-specific features of problems (65). It is possible to see the differences between novice and experienced tutors in these terms—as an expert tutor, I could decide that it was acceptable to veer from normal practice to proofread that last-minute grant proposal, whereas a novice tutor would have been more likely to refuse. Still, there is something about these definitions that doesn't quite fit what writing centers do.

Perhaps the problem is not an inability to identify writing-center expertise but an unwillingness to be associated with a kind of expertise that writing-center specialists find problematic. If, as Geisler reports, there are two different ways of looking at expertise—one that valorizes expertise as a cognitive achievement and one that critiques expertise as the source of many of the ills in Western society—many writing-center folks would gladly put themselves in the second camp. Here is another part of the professional identity of most writing-center workers: they are people who try to break down hierarchies between those who know and those who don't. Geisler herself argues that the "cultural movement of professionalization has used the technology of literacy to sustain claims to professional privilege, creating a *great divide* between expert and layperson" (xiii). It is not surprising, then, that writing-center workers would resist such professionalization. For indeed, they often take pleasure in identifying themselves as operating outside of the typical institutional hierarchy that dictates relationships between experts and novices. Even when tutors have more advanced academic credentials than the writers they work with, they are encouraged to create a peerlike relationship between fellow writers. In some respects, then, it could be said that they are experts in not appearing to be experts. But it is exactly this reluctance to claim disciplinary expertise that can lead others to perceive writing centers as serving the needs of other disciplines rather than their own disciplinary agenda.

Ironically, one of the first compositionists to advocate collaborative learning, Kenneth Bruffee (1984), believed that by working in peer groups, with the guidance of a teacher, students could learn to write in ways associated with academic expertise. Although Bruffee's claims for the efficacy of peer learning have been embraced by the writing-center community, his focus on acculturating students into the academy's "normal" ways of knowing and writing has also been criticized by many writing-center personnel who wish to problematize the normalizing effect of the academy. As Dave Healy puts it in his essay "A Defense of Dualism" (1993), regardless of where writing centers are actually located, their metaphorical location is and should remain outside of the classroom: "The writing center is a place, and a place with political as well as metaphorical status" (179).

More than a decade ago, Harvey Kail and John Trimbur (1987) made a similar distinction between writing-center work that supports the traditional hierarchy between experts and novices and the kind of writing center positioned outside the classroom where students are asked "to rely on themselves, to learn on their own in the absence of faculty authority figures or their surrogates" (207). For Kail and Trimbur, collaborative learning provides the means by which students can "reinterpret the power of the faculty, and to see that their own autonomous colearning constitutes the practical source of knowledge" (208). According to Marilyn Cooper (1994), undergraduate peer tutors are particularly well suited for leading students to a critical understanding of academic discourse and a means of achieving agency within it. Because of their position as students who are not academic professionals, these peer tutors "have little investment in disciplinary beliefs and practices, and they are thus less responsive to its standards and expectations than they are to the needs and experiences of their peers" (144).

Writing centers, then, may consider themselves experts in collaboration, but toward what end—the acculturation of students into academic norms or the interrogation of academic hierarchy? The answer to this question has special implications for graduate students and the tutors who work with them. It may be tempting to assume that graduate students are already acculturated into the academy or are at least firmly committed to a continuing mastery of the "normal" discourse of their field. Ironically, Linda Shamoon and Deborah Burns (1995) argue, in "A Critique of Pure Tutoring," that because graduate students *lack* expertise in the kind of scholarly writing expected of them, they can especially benefit from explicit instruction in how to gain that authority. For Burns and many of the faculty she and Shamoon talked with, mastery of disciplinary writing resulted from direct instruction and sometimes intrusive intervention by more knowledgeable practitioners, usually the faculty supervising their graduate work. As Burns describes it, her director was "directive, he substituted his own words for hers, and he stated with disciplinary appropriateness the ideas with which she had been working" (138). The authors acknowledge that what Burns' professor did "violated current composition orthodoxy. His practices seem authoritative, intrusive, directive, and product-oriented," and yet, according to Burns, this kind of intervention "made knowledge and achievement accessible" (138).

Shamoon and Burns recommend that writing centers become sites "where directive tutoring provides a sheltered and protected time and space for practice that leads to the accumulation of important repertoires, the expression of new social identities, and the articulation of domain-appropriate rhetoric" (147). Specifically, they suggest that writing centers bring in experts to help make public, through directive tutoring and modeling, the discipline-specific writing strategies typically hidden from novices. Judith Powers (1995) describes a similar model of "bringing in the expert" that seems to place writing centers in an unproblematic position as a supporter of academic norms. In Powers' "trialogue" model, the graduate student's advisor is formally invited into the tutorial process and is given the chance to "discuss his/her perception of where the student is in the writing process and what the director hopes will come out of our conference with that student" (15). Powers emphasizes that all three members of the trialogue are important: "The advisor brings the expectations of the discipline . . . the writing center brings knowledge of the writing process and . . . collaborative learning methods . . . and the writer brings the research topic, data, and relevant analysis" (15). In this scenario, each person's expertise is validated.

It is logical to assume that graduate students would benefit from more explicit instruction about the rhetoric of scholarly writing in particular disciplines, but unfortunately, many faculty seem unable or unwilling to provide such instruction. As Pat Sullivan (1994) found in her study of graduate students in English, most were expected to write literary criticism without being taught how to do so. Many faculty may not themselves have been taught to read and to write scholarly prose, making it difficult for them to teach what they now know tacitly. Geisler (1994) notes that, in the current system of education, expertise has been formally separated into domain knowledge and rhetorical knowledge. As a consequence, novices may have access to domain knowledge without access to rhetorical knowledge. Not surprisingly, social and cultural critiques of professionalization identify these practices as intentionally exclusionary. Those who have managed to learn the ropes and to achieve the status of experts have a vested interest in limiting that expertise, thus maintaining both their own intellectual and material status as well as the continued demand for their services (Geisler 1994).

This feeling of being excluded from essential rhetorical knowledge certainly characterizes the experience of one of the graduate students who visited my writing center regularly throughout the three years she was working on her master's degree. Although she claimed to have learned a lot about writing from her various writing-center tutors, she still wished her department had offered a course in how to write scholarly papers in her field. As she put it, "There are so many things they could do to ease the pain. What they end up doing is saying, 'Well, you're just not cut out to do this.'" Writing-center tutors can attempt to address graduate students' need for rhetorical knowledge by analyzing with them examples of published articles and completed theses in the field. Tutors may also offer direct instruction. One tutor I observed working with Marguerite discussed with her the characteristics of an acceptable thesis, the appropriate scope for a seminar paper, readers' needs in terms of signposts, as well as time-honored means of organizing complex information. He also created a handout that showed how to organize a paper in a comparison-contrast format, which he used to encourage her to move beyond merely inventing ideas to think about how she should present them for readers.

In the examples I've just described, tutors seemed to position themselves as advocates of academic writing who help graduate student writers comply with established norms. But for some graduate students, their goals of becoming accomplished writers and bona fide knowledge makers in their chosen fields can be inhibited by mandates to comply with existing discourse conventions. This seems especially true for those who do not feel "at home" in the university or for those who may be asking unconventional questions about unconventional subjects. As one of the tutors described the graduate students he's worked with, "They're traumatized by their departments. It's like they've been beaten up by their department." Mary, a master's student in art history, was discouraged from following her interest in the patronage system behind painted Japanese screens because there wasn't adequate evidence. However, she continued to talk about her interests with her writing-center tutors. When a trip to Japan resulted in a serendipitous meeting with a Japanese scholar who had published an article on the patronage of the screen she was studying, her faculty director grudgingly allowed her to include references to this scholar's work. When Debbie took to her director the draft of her thesis that she'd worked on in the writing center over several semesters and was told she should have hired an editor, she returned to the writing center to share her frustration and anger. In violation of the unwritten rule never to criticize faculty, one tutor wryly noted that the students who were having difficulty getting their work accepted were all returning women. Emboldened with this new perspective on her situation, Debbie phoned me to ask for advice in dealing with her professor, commenting, "He's just doing this to make me want to quit, but I'm not quitting."

Although tutors working with graduate students may provide direct instruction in academic conventions, they also provide cogent critiques of the academic institution's exclusionary practices, perhaps because as would-be experts themselves, they have seen and experienced these practices. Graduate students who seek help in the writing center need to know that their ideas are interesting and valid, especially when the responses they receive from their faculty make them question their ability. As one tutor put it, "It's almost like they're trying to get their bearings, and they want somebody to say, like, I'm not insane. That's what Marguerite wanted me to tell her, that she's not crazy, first of all, and that her ideas aren't stupid." Indeed, based on this study, I have decided to maintain my policy of not contacting a graduate student's major professor even though most know that their students are working with us. Given the uneasy relationship some of these students have with academic authority—and occasionally with the particular faculty member in authority over them—it seems important to remain positioned as a student advocate, free from any direct obligation to fulfill faculty members' expectations. Certainly there are times when tutors recommend that graduate students take specific questions back to their professors, but that move seems politically different from inviting the professor to set the agenda.

In "Migrant Rationalities: Graduate Students and the Idea of Authority in the Writing Center," Nancy Welch (1995) also considers the problem that academic authority poses for some graduate students. Welch describes three graduate students who were stifled in their writing by a belief that their only choice was to accommodate or to resist disciplinary conventions. According to Welch's reading of these cases, each student gained a sense of authority when their tutors encouraged them to interrogate and play with seemingly fixed notions of what constitutes authority in various fields, activities that put these students on the path to revising "their constructions of authority from some out-there package to something they make and remake in writing" (6). In this model, the writing center is not explicitly allied with conventional disciplinary authority, as in Powers' *trialogue* model, nor outside of and opposed to it, as in Healy's defense of classroom–writing center dualism. Instead, Welch describes her model of the writing center as "not an either/or crossroads but a busy, noisy, fascinating intersection" where conventional forms of academic authority are acknowledged but also challenged (19). Ultimately, however, as Welch notes in her conclusion, most graduate students cannot afford to abandon the forms of academic writing that mark one as an expert. Though playfulness and reverie may work well as invention or revision techniques, they are unlikely to result in drastic changes in students' notions of what is ultimately expected of them. As Grimm (1996) points out, because writing centers are ultimately located in and financed by institutions, "a contestatory practice will not work for writing centers" (541). Indeed, my advice to Debbie who was having trouble with her director was to ask him to tell her exactly what he wanted her to do and to write it down, so he'd know she took his recommendations seriously.

What role, then, can and should writing centers play in the process of professionalizing graduate students, of turning novices into experts? What do they have to offer students like Marguerite? Certainly writing centers can offer graduate students the same benefits that they offer undergraduates. Writing centers do have expertise in grammar, in writer-centered, collaborative teaching practices, in the rhetorical analysis of disciplinary conventions, and in the critique of academic institutions. But my study reveals one more important service that writing centers provide graduate students, a service that has proven especially valuable to students like Marguerite, now in her third year of working with us. Writing centers provide an opportunity for graduate students to build relationships with other writers, relationships based on conversations about ideas and about writing that might be seen as rehearsals of expertise, rehearsals staged for the benefit of a nonevaluative but intelligent and engaged audience of one. And the performance goes on in both directions: both writer and tutor are performing their expertise and receiving a response. Based on my ongoing conversations with these graduate students, I have come to accept completely Grimm's (1996) admonition that "writing centers need to focus on Vygotsky's strongest conclusion—that language is learned by participating in human relationships, not by sitting on the sidelines and listening to the rules being explained" (535). The language of expertise is learned by performing that expertise.

Although this focus on the importance of relationships to learning represents orthodox writing-center practice, the literature on graduate students in the writing center tends to shift the focus from relationships to the specter of expert knowledge. Writing centers are in a special position to provide not expert knowledge per se but rather support for the knower and the process of knowing through the cultivation of relationships. Tutors themselves touted these relationships as one of the most intellectually demanding yet rewarding parts of working in the writing center. As one tutor noted, "You have to spend a lot more time with a graduate student getting to know them . . . and it's much more important for a graduate student to get to know you. . . . They want to know who you are and where you're coming from to see if they're going to be compatible working with you. . . . You really have to develop much more of a bond of trust with graduate students." Another tutor remarked, "You have to want to be involved in their project. If you don't, this [kind of tutoring] is not for you. It's really not fair to them. . . . Be willing to draw on your own experience. Share your own personal struggles with them. Be open enough to make them feel like they're not alone. Because that's one of the worst parts about graduate work is that isolation. No one's doing the exact same project. You're working very much alone. You feel like no one else understands this so it helps to be willing to step out of that role of, like, teacher."

Letting the graduate student play the role of teacher—of rehearsing their expertise—is clearly an important part of the relationship. Jackie, an experienced tutor, admitted that she told one of her graduate students during their first tutorial that she did not know anything about the student's field, a move that can be risky given graduate students' valorization of expertise. Yet Jackie's yielding of the stage to the student proved to be advantageous to this student's development as an expert: "I would say, 'Okay, just stop. Talk to me. Talk your paper to me.' So it became much more productive because I didn't know the material and she could synthesize it better when she could talk about it. She had to explain it to me. . . . For me it was the model learning situation. I was learning so much from her about how to put together this piece and also a lot about art history. . . . So it was neat because we would switch roles that I don't think we have the opportunity to do with other students." Of course the tutor's expertise is an important part of the equation as well. Carla reported, "The graduate student I'm working with now, he trusts my insights. And he feels like, not just that I'm an expert on writing, but he feels that I'm an intelligent person. He values my opinion. You have to be a thinker. And to take risks, say 'I don't understand.' You have to be willing to learn and not be afraid of your own ego that you're supposed to know everything, because it's obvious that I still know most about the writing, but it's an intellectual process; it's a give and take." And Jackie confirmed the level of commitment and energy required to maintain these productive relationships with graduate students: "What I didn't expect was the level of intensity. And that I would have to be on my toes the whole time."

What the writing center has to offer a student like Marguerite, then, is this kind of intense, intellectual relationship, one in which she gets some help with her writing and shares her professional expertise with her tutors as well. Indeed, after spending every term of her three years of graduate study enrolled in the writing center, Marguerite pulled me aside to assure me that she was not taking advantage of our services, that she benefited immensely from the opportunity to talk through her ideas, especially since no one in her department was an expert in what she was working on. She had even begun to contemplate doing Ph.D. work in comparative literature. As one of her former tutors commented, "She is one of the rare students who really believes in what she's doing and really is exploring an interest and chasing it down and getting all the information, so it's good to see that she's getting some satisfaction out of that."

I don't know that it is any less difficult to explain writing-center expertise in terms of this building of intellectual relationships between emerging experts. But if knowledge making is akin to conversation, and if language learning is ultimately relational, then it stands to reason that writing centers should be at the *center* of the professionalization enterprise, not haunted by their lack of expert knowledge and not beholden to the expertise of others, but actively engaged in the production of experts poised to share new knowledge with the world.

Works Cited

Bruffee, K. A. [1984] 1995. "Peer Tutoring and the 'Conversation of Mankind.'" In *Landmark Essays on Writing Centers,* edited by C. Murphy and J. Law, 87–99. Davis, CA: Hermagoras.

Cooper, M. M. 1994. "Really Useful Knowledge: A Cultural Studies Agenda for Writing Centers." *The Writing Center Journal* 14 (2): 97–111.

Geisler, C. 1994. *Academic Literacy and the Nature of Expertise: Reading, Writing, and Knowing in Academic Philosophy.* Hillsdale, NJ: Erlbaum.

Grimm, N. M. 1996. "Rearticulating the Work of the Writing Center." *College Composition and Communication* 47 (4): 523–48.

Harris, M. 1995. "Talking in the Middle: Why Writers Need Writing Tutors." *College English* 57 (1): 27–42.

Healy, D. [1993] 1995. "A Defense of Dualism: The Writing-Center and the Classroom." In *Landmark Essays on Writing Centers,* edited by C. Murphy and J. Law, 179–90. Davis, CA: Hermagoras.

Kail, H., and J. Trimbur. [1987] 1995. "The Politics of Peer Tutoring." In *Landmark Essays on Writing Centers,* edited by C. Murphy and J. Law, 203–10. Davis, CA: Hermagoras.

North. S. 1984. "The Idea of a Writing Center." *College English* 46 (5): 433–46.

————. 1994. "Revisiting 'The Idea of a Writing Center.'" *The Writing Center Journal* 15 (1): 7–19.

Powers, J. K. 1995. "Assisting the Graduate Thesis Writer Through Faculty and Writing Center Collaboration." *Writing Lab Newsletter* 20 (2): 13–16.

Shamoon, L. K., and D. Burns. 1995. "A Critique of Pure Tutoring." *The Writing Center Journal* 15 (2): 134–51.

Sullivan, P. A. 1994. "Writing in the Graduate Curriculum: Literary Criticism as Composition." In *Composition Theory for the Postmodern Classroom,* edited by G. A. Olson and S. I. Dobrin, 32–48. Albany: State University of New York Press.

Welch, N. 1995. "Migrant Rationalities: Graduate Students and the Idea of Authority in the Writing Center." *The Writing Center Journal* 16 (1): 5–23.

6

Labor Pains

A Political Analysis of Writing Center Tutoring

Linda K. Shamoon and Deborah H. Burns

Writing-center scholarship of the past fifteen years includes a stream of discourse lamenting the shabby working conditions, the low pay, and the lack of faculty and/or professional status for tutors and directors, as well as a general lack of understanding and respect for the mission of the writing center. These lamentations are often, ironically, accompanied by a sense of pride in the marginalization of writing centers. Indeed, there seems to be an ethos of rugged individualism celebrated by many writing centers, seeing the facility as the last bastion of independence in an institution that otherwise pressures for conformity, and maintaining that the marginalized position offers tutors and tutees a space for a special kind of work and critical vision. For example, Judith Summerfield (1988) valorizes the peeled paint and worn couches of writing centers, and suggests writing centers should maintain their marginalization as central to their philosophy and mission. Terrance Riley (1994) states that writing centers should work to maintain their outsider status and "acknowledge that directing a writing center does not involve the kind of difficulties for which an advanced degree preparation is necessary" (31–32). Riley goes on to say that writing-center energy "at present derives from what we have left of happy amateurism" (32). John Trimbur (1987), in discussing who is best suited to do the work of tutoring, argues that the nonexpert tutor is the best. His implication is that the outsider, the stranger, may be the best suited to ask questions that will make authors look again at their texts and prompt them to rethink critically their underlying assumption. In this kind of writing-center discourse we see repeated attempts to glorify those circumstances that make writing-center work stressful because an often shabby or understaffed facility supposedly offers both sanctuary and a critical perspective on the larger institution and its hegemonic modes of thought.

We are suspicious of these rationalizations. We fear that such discourse leads to the accommodation of writing-center staff and leadership to their present unfair circumstances, and we believe that adherence to such reasoning will close rather than open the discipline's critical eye to its bounded or narrow practices and ways of thinking. While there is much to celebrate in writing-center achievement, we cannot valorize its marginality. Rather, we see this marginality as a constant prod to examine and resist those circumstances—both material and cultural—that hold the center to its current position. Instead of valorizing the current position of the writing center, we argue that the various aspects of the "labor" in writing centers are laid bare by a neo-Marxist perspective on work within the academy that forces the discipline to question everyday habits in writing centers. First, we want to explain elements of this perspective and then trace the ways in which we see these elements shaping writing-center labor.

A Critical Perspective on Writing-Center Labor

It is reasonable to look at the modern American university as a site of labor and production, and since the late 1800s this education institution has been dedicated in part to training and graduating—in short, producing—the scientists, engineers, and technicians of an industrial society, as well as to educating the middle and upper classes for citizenry in a democratic society. While these two missions sometimes find themselves in conflict within the institution, they nevertheless constitute much of the work of the modern academy. This kind of education work may be conducted in any number of ways, but in America it is inevitably influenced by Fordist concepts of production, particularly the breaking apart of complex tasks into their simplest units of work in order to make possible large-scale production of easily reproducible parts, and the creating of easily filled slots for labor. Some of the many effects of this mode of labor and production include an emphasis on the standardization of parts and labor, the maximization of efficiency along with the elimination of any duplication of tasks or work, and the maximization of profits particularly by attempting to drive down the costs of labor and materials. Marx and an array of post-Marxian theorists, especially Antonio Gramsci and Louis Althusser, have shown that such a system must be held in place by both a class structure and a complex of ideas and institutions that organize the world so that the economic and class arrangements seem inevitable, natural, without alternatives, and even beneficial to the society as a whole (see Marx 1993; Eagleton 1991; Coward and Ellis 1977).

To some extent, the contemporary university is caught up in these economic, social, and ideological imperatives. The university has an array of products, including its graduates, its publications and research, its service functions to the larger or linked communities, and so on. The university also has workers, including all of the academic and nonacademic staff, and it faces severe economic conditions that constrain it to work not for profit but for a balanced accounting of income and expenditures that can often come about only through a struggle for wider sources of money. These additional resources must be gained through the "surplus value" generated by the university's star faculty, athletic teams, loyal alumni, and institutional links to other religious or social institutions. In response to this stress, the university struggles to be productively efficient through an array of means, for example, by eliminating overlaps and duplication in its curriculum, by maximizing the number of students assigned to classes and instructors, by eliminating or restructuring programs that do not reach a certain level of "productivity," by limiting or reducing the numbers of its most expensive laborers (its tenured faculty), and by using whenever possible nontenured, inexpensive labor (part-timers, lecturers, graduate and undergraduate students). That all of this seems necessary and inevitable is a perspective held in place by an array of beliefs and social arrangements, such as that the university must be held to the same levelheaded principles of accounting as any business, that efficiency during production will lead to a better or cheaper product, and so on.

The contemporary writing center is in many ways enmeshed in these circumstances and ways of thinking. For example, even though writing-center work could be done by a wide array of individuals including the tenured professor, in the modern, Fordist university it will be done by the lowest-paid and least-skilled worker. The fact that generalist tutoring has a reasonable rationale and often helps improve a piece of writing does not negate the fact that the writing center's labor arrangements fit smoothly, even opportunistically, within the modern university's willingness to hire a certain kind of labor whenever possible, namely part-timers and graduate students, and if possible to hire even lesser-expert or lower-status workers, namely undergraduate tutors. Also, as we will argue below, the daily work these laborers perform may feel varied from appointment to appointment, but in truth it is standardized and reduces the focus on writing primarily to text-in-hand, author-centered expression of unified statements in a manner that can be dealt with in a session of twenty to thirty minutes. Such reductivist conversations about writing do offer some support for the improvement of a text in progress, but they hardly cover the full range of writing instruction. We are struck by the way in which this standardized, generalist tutoring fits into the labor circumstances of the modern university.

We are arguing not that writing-center pedagogy is deliberately capitalistic or repressive, but merely that there is a coming together of needs and circumstances that serve the productivity of both the university and the center. In our view, this is not necessarily bad, especially if both organizations serve their workers and clients fairly, justly, and fruitfully. However, when these conditions become entrenched or shift to reveal forms of exploitation, stressful conflict, or underlying ideological orientations that irrationally constrict the modes of work, then we would call the opportunistic relationship complicit in establishing or maintaining a harmful status quo. We would like to explore two ways in which the university and the writing center are harmfully complicit: in the construction of the work of tutoring, and in the glorification of a low-skill labor pool that derives from and is supported by that construction.

The Construction of the Work of Tutoring

Writing-center construction of the work of tutoring implicates the center in the Fordist approach to production, even though the daily work of helping writers seems to offer the tutors an array of challenges and satisfactions that prevent a general feeling of alienation. With each new student who walks in the door bringing a unique combination of issues concerning writing, tutoring work seems like it should be nonstandardized, even creative, and unified with its objective—helping students to improve as writers. However, the extensive instructional literature on how to tutor writing has served to standardize that work, making it uniform, repetitive, bounded, and inexpert, while the discourse in the scholarly literature about tutoring extends and constantly reinscribes this narrowly constructed portrait of such labor.

The standardization of tutoring writing is most obviously revealed in the sequence of behaviors and topics of discussion that is officially described and sanctioned in tutoring manuals, as well as in these manuals' avoidance of other topics and instructional methods. In various tutoring guides, the tutor is advised to begin a session with questions about the assignment, about the goals of the paper, about how far along the student is in writing the paper, and about where the student wants to go with the paper (Clark 1998; Ryan 1994; Meyer and Smith 1987). Any of these questions might generate enough talk for the student to feel ready to revise the paper. If that is the case, the tutor may turn to the next client's draft, starting with the same questions and moving through the same issues.

Of course, any session may move beyond this opening routine, but there are narrowly predictable aspects of writing that will be covered. The session may move on to looking at the student's text to see how well the paper expresses the author's intentions, and may give feedback aimed at helping the student identify which passages may need clarifying and how to engage in such revision. In a session like this, although the student may enter the center ready to discuss certain, sometimes troubling topics, the tutor is advised not to talk about the specific or difficult circumstances of the class or the assignment, and certainly not to evaluate the instructor or the feedback given by the instructor. In addition, tutors may not resort to more direct teaching, such as modeling ways to write, and in many centers tutors may not write on students' papers or directly address how a particular discipline, class, or specific teacher may want the writing to be. In fact, in some circumstances, tutors who have taken the same class or know the subject matter may not be allowed to tutor students in those classes (Haring-Smith 1992). Finally, many tutors may not know what to do with students who enter the center without a paper in progress, and in many instances grammar instruction may be outside the boundaries of acceptable tutoring practice. Thus, a certain kind of tutoring has a certain kind of routine, addressing some issues in writing and not others, setting boundaries, and separating tutors from some parts of the writing experience while privileging other parts.

This kind of tutoring has been labeled *generalist tutoring* because it can be applied to writing in general by anyone who has received guidance from tutoring manuals. That is, no matter what kind of writing is called for, no matter what the writing situation is, no matter how skilled, experienced, or knowledgeable the writer or tutor is about subject matter, genre, or context, the generalist approach can be invoked, for it draws on one set of issues regarding writing, and it appears to call for no particular expertise regarding subject matter, specific writing structures, formats or contexts, rhetoric, grammar, or other selected elements of writing. Instead, it may draw upon a set of personal qualities and interpersonal skills that are often labeled friendly, supportive, nurturing, and responsive, and upon an operative familiarity with steps in the writing process. Obviously, not everyone has such traits or operative knowledge, but in our centers and in several we have observed, after a selection process to identify appropriate tutors, and after some training-and-observation sessions about drafting and revising papers and about interacting with authors, generalist tutors may start their work. We cannot avoid the conclusion that this is a low-skilled approach to improving writing. We recognize that many centers may not operate in this manner, that they conduct much longer training periods, and that they attempt to professionalize tutoring practices in a number of ways. However, this does not deny the fact that it is quite possible to conduct a generalist-tutoring center based on low-skilled labor and that many centers (maybe most) do so.

We want to make a final point about this construction of tutoring work. Within writing-center culture this construction is maintained by a structure of scholarly discourse. All tutoring manuals explain generalist tutoring, and they have derived their guidelines from the discourse of academic publications, which either justifies further iterations of generalist tutoring, presents personal, positive testimonies as "findings" from studies about generalist tutoring, or rationalizes the problematic conflicts or issues that arise from generalist tutoring (such as conflicts that arise from charges of plagiarism). The effect is that one kind of tutoring is promulgated, studied, explained, examined, improved, and then promulgated once again. This situation demonstrates Anthony Giddens' (1993) theme that the dominant discourse both maintains a set of practices and reproduces the larger social structure in which it is inscribed. In addition, following both Gramsci and Althusser, this discourse hegemonizes a certain kind of tutoring as natural and without reasonable alternative. Discourse about other kinds of tutoring seems either off-limits or odd. In the wider discipline of composition studies, of course, there are other perspectives on writing, such as writing within academic contexts, or writing as learning about and gaining entry to a profession, or writing based on other rhetorical situations. Each of these perspectives is viable within higher education, and each might lead to different ways of tutoring done by a different pool of labor in a different relationship to the context, the writing, and the author. In other words, diversity in writing-center culture is imaginable and reasonable but not talked about or available. Given this situation, we argue that writing centers' ideological construction of the work of tutoring is complicit in maintaining the daily work of tutoring as low-skilled and standardized. Such labor finds a place in a Fordist university, but it is also held in place—its marginal place—by that construction.

The Effect on Writing-Center Workers

Before offering a cautionary tale about trying to diversify and break out of this construction of writing-center labor, we want to explore a closely related aspect of laboring in the writing center. This aspect pertains to the stress that results from the conflicted conditions in which writing-center workers labor. We argue that the dependence of writing centers upon generalist tutoring not only helps to hold centers on the margins of academia, but it contributes to the stress that is deleterious to all of the centers' workers in the long run.

When we look at the history of our own writing centers at the University of Rhode Island and at Merrimack College, we acknowledge that these facilities got started because their use of low-paid labor had little impact on the budgets of our institutions. In each case, our centers started on a budgetary shoestring, and through the dedicated work of part-timers and nontenured instructors, a certain amount of support for students and their writing became available. Over the years, our two writing centers have flourished in terms of increased student use, increased recognition on campus, better furniture, locations, and equipment, and more staff members. But until recently, these centers did little to try to change the portrait of tutoring as a generalist endeavor that may be learned by anyone to help anyone. As a result, our centers have remained vulnerable to being pushed out of the academic endeavors of the institution, precisely because the tutoring does not seem to be academic (in the admittedly narrow use of that term). In fact, in the Division of Continuing Education at URI the writing center has been changed into a learning-skills center, and on the main campus some faculty are pushing for the use of undergraduates rather than graduate student tutors because of the low level of the work. Thus, these centers' workers—including the tenure-line directors—always labor under this vulnerability. This is the most unfortunate aspect of our complicity with the labor circumstances of the larger institution. Furthermore, we do not think our centers are atypical of many around the country.

The point we want to emphasize is that writing-center laborers are in a conflicted position in part because of the generalist construction of the nature of their work (although there are many other forces at play, too). The generalist construction was one of the several factors that helped to give these facilities their start, but it remains in place while writing-center leaders try to build a secure future for their facilities and promote a discipline-based view of their work. In writing-center culture the push toward stability has been synonymous with the push to professionalize, and the push to professionalize has taken many forms, including the institution of training programs for tutors, the continued alliance of its operations with rhetoric and composition studies, and the development of its own professional group, research journal, and newsletter. Thus, within the culture of writing centers there has developed a belief in the need for disciplinary expertise in order to do high-quality tutoring work, and there has emerged a special identity that binds writing-center workers to an academic endeavor—the study of writing—that has a teaching and a research function. Unfortunately, in many instances these elements of professionalism flourish only within the cultural milieu of the center, and they are in conflict with the wider institutional and popular culture's view that helping students improve their writing is remedial work or nonacademic study-skills work. This outsider-versus-insider perception tears away at the conditions of labor in the center, holding in place a conflict that is exacerbated by the central role of standardized generalist tutoring.

Our portrait of the center's conflicted laborer is best observed in the situation of the director, especially if the director has a tenure-track position. The tenure-line appointment usually indicates a recognition of the academic value of the facility, and the mere candidacy for tenure means the director, at least, is not at the edges of status, security, and power as are the other center workers. Typically, however, in everyday practice many center directors suffer severe stress or conflict because the demands of directing (such as training a staff to work in disciplinary and research-based ways, running the facility in a just manner, and communicating with faculty about the nature and quality of the work of the center) are simply not seen by other members of the department or the administration as being part of the intellectual work of the academy (Healy 1995). At the same time, these directorial activities leave little time for the more standard forms of intellectual academic work, particularly disciplinary research and journal publishing. Furthermore, when directors do engage in this kind of intellectual work, it often is, and should be, about the work of the center, a topic that may not have the cachet of a literary scholar's analysis of a sixteenth-century poem. Thus, the director, perhaps more than any other worker in the center, may be said to occupy a marginalized position—if *marginalized* is defined as it was originally used by sociologists Robert E. Park and Everett Stonequist (Pavalko 1988, 42). They argue that a marginalized position within a social system is one that traps individuals between communities that have conflicting sets of values, making it difficult for the individual to take meaningful action or achieve a fully realized identity within either social sphere, while placing responsibility for action and self-realization squarely upon the individual. This is precisely the predicament of writing-center directors.

What we see as a primary commonality among centers is that their laborers are caught in problematic, conflicted positions at the edges of academic structures. Most are temporary workers; some, quite frankly, long to be otherwise situated in the institution; and many are without the power or status to alter the general perception that the work they are doing is remedial. The one institutional "insider," the director, may be the most conflicted and stressed among all of the laborers. We realize that writing programs, too, suffer many of the same problems, and that no department or university can escape the Fordist conditions of academic culture. Our argument in this essay is that writing-center leaders and scholars should try to recognize and reduce those elements of their own practice that may be complicit with the overall tendency to reduce, limit, and standardize writing-center work, and that may intensify the forces that debilitate the workers. In our view it is time to recognize that an ideological adherence to one kind of tutoring plays a major role in this complicity.

A Cautionary Tale

We want to conclude this essay with a cautionary tale. It is the story of one center's attempt to diversify its tutoring practices and in this way to move off the margins of its institution's operational arrangements. At Merrimack College, Burns deliberately shifted that center's theoretical perspective regarding the tutoring of writing. She turned to a rhetorical perspective, she acknowledged the importance of models and scaffolding in the learning of new skills, and she integrated these factors into a different approach toward tutoring. As she developed this approach, she found herself moving toward a set of tutoring practices that are, in many ways, dialectically opposed to generalist tutoring, and are, in spite of discourse to the contrary, very exciting. These changes seemed to prompt an array of other changes regarding this center's political position in the institution, especially in giving more status and recognition to writing tutors and to writing in general, although they did not free this center from the politics that still surround writing in academia and in a Fordist culture.

The first change that came with a shift away from generalist tutoring concerned a change in who tutors—who labors—in the center. At Merrimack the "dedicated" or "near-expert" tutor is replacing the generalist tutor. The near-expert tutors, unlike the generalist tutors, have some knowledge about the area of study, the writing assignments, and perhaps even about the classes to which they are assigned. They may have taken the class, or be a major in the discipline, or have some experience in writing the kinds of papers asked for in the class. Furthermore, the near-expert tutor may be dedicated to that one class as its writing tutor. Thus, instead of being "contained" in the center's facility, dedicated tutors are assigned to specific classes where writing assignments will be given. They are usually present in the classroom, and they are aware of the class's writing assignments, their specific context, and the specific audience, namely the teacher and how that teacher reads. In conferences with instructors, the near-expert tutors are encouraged to interrogate the instructor, to ask about the *why, how,* and *what* of the assignments—and how these will be evaluated—and to suggest clearer ways these may be transmitted to the students in the class. In conferences with students, their talk is still on drafting and revising, but because the tutor knows the discipline and more of its ways of writing, there is a closer relationship between discussion of the subject matter in the class and the ways these topics are approached and framed in writing. Also, because the tutor knows the classroom, the teacher, and the assignments, and because the instructor has endorsed the tutor's role as facilitator in that classroom, the tutor and student writers are allowed to discuss the demands and expectations of the specific audience. Yet the tutor is still a student and remains a companion in exploring the difficulties, frustrations, and impenetrability of this new disciplinary territory. Thus the tutoring is more focused but also more wide-ranging, varied, and under the control of the tutor.

At Merrimack, then, with the embracing of rhetorical principles and disciplinary discourse, different people are tutoring in a different way. We know that such an approach has been opposed in writing-center scholarship, and we have much to say about these issues. In this essay, however, we want to focus on how diversifying tutoring practices has played out politically for this center. One part of this tale includes happy episodes. In the wake of the changes in tutoring practice, the use of the writing center increased by more than 300 percent. More students used the center, more faculty from across the curriculum became engaged in aspects of the tutoring process, especially in discussing writing assignments with tutors and with the center's director, and, overall, the reputation of the center improved. The center, with an increased budget, became more integral to the intellectual life of that academic community.

On the other hand, the writing center at Merrimack College has remained vulnerable to administrative and economic forces within the institution. The change in tutoring practice did not convince everyone that such work must include some degree of expertise and that to be effective such work must be wide ranging and high level. There remain at Merrimack several administrators and a few faculty members who continue to believe that the writing center should concentrate on the "basics" of student texts and that the center should place more focus on correcting grammar and punctuation. They continue to insist that tutoring writing requires no special or disciplinary knowledge, and that student writing needs can be served more efficiently by nonexpert tutors in a general study skills center. Furthermore, even though Merrimack's writing center focuses on discipline-specific tutoring, some faculty do not understand the value of the rhetorical training given writing-center tutors, and some believe they are more qualified to train tutors of writing within their fields. This faculty believes that tutoring should take place within departments rather than be organized in a central location with tutors trained by faculty from the English department. In addition, while expert tutors may be valued and desired by many faculty, they are not necessarily seen as indispensable by administrators who know little about what goes on in a writing center. And in the end, we too have to admit that while the shift to using expert tutors has been a major step inside the discipline, Merrimack's writing center still uses low-paid, lesser-status employees for difficult, stressful work. In a Fordist institution, however, which is itself situated within a culture in which writing is merely basic, we have learned that it may be nearly impossible to completely overcome the politics of writing centers.

Conclusion

We have argued that writing centers are products of their histories and circumstances, and that their own construction of their labor reveals a lot about where they are institutionally. An approach toward writing that depends upon generalist tutors helps writing centers flourish in a market-driven educational institution. At the same time, this universally employed tutor may reinforce the message that writing assistance is a regrettably necessary, low-level service. Thus, some of the conditions of history and circumstance have helped the center to grow, but these same circumstances may now be holding centers in thrall. By contrast, the center at Merrimack consciously examined and shifted the perspective on writing, and this move has changed what it does and who does it. This approach improved the center's position in the institution, even if it did not entirely change the culture in which writing instruction occurs. We do not know if the outcome would be similar at other places, but we suggest that it is time for writing-center leaders and scholars to be more self-conscious of what it is they adhere to philosophically and what the consequences in terms of everyday practices are. Perhaps it is time in writing-center scholarship to make the familiar strange.

Works Cited

Clark, I. 1998. *Writing in the Center: Teaching in a Writing Center Setting.* 3d ed. Dubuque, IA: Kendall/Hunt.

Coward, R., and J. Ellis. 1977. "Marxism, Language, and Ideology." In *Language and Materialism: Developments in Semiology and the Theory of the Subject.* London: Routledge and Paul.

Eagleton, T. 1991. "From Lukacs to Gramsci." In *Ideology: An Introduction.* London: Verso.

Giddens, A. 1993. "Critical Theory." In *The Giddens Reader*, edited by P. Cassell. Stanford, CA: Stanford University Press.

Haring-Smith, T. 1992. "Changing Students' Attitudes: Writing Fellows Program." In *Writing Across the Curriculum: A Guide to Developing Programs*, edited by S. H. McLeod and M. Soven, 177–78. Newbury Park, CA: Sage Publications.

Healy, D. 1995. "Writing Center Directors: An Emerging Portrait of the Profession." *WPA: Writing Program Administration* 18 (3): 26–43.

Marx, K. 1993. *Wage Labour and Capital*. New York: International Publishers.

Meyer, E., and L. Smith. 1987. *The Practical Tutor*. New York: Oxford University Press.

Pavalko, R. M. 1988. *Sociology of Occupations and Professions*. 2d ed. Itasca, IL: F. E. Peacock.

Riley, T. 1994. "The Unpromising Future of Writing Centers." *The Writing Center Journal* 15 (1): 20–34.

Ryan, L. 1994. *The Bedford Guide for Writing Tutors*. Boston: Bedford Books/St. Martin's.

Summerfield, J. [1988] 1995. "Writing Centers: A Long View." In *Landmark Essays on Writing Centers*, edited by C. Murphy and J. Law, 63–68. Davis, CA: Hermagoras.

Trimbur, J. 1987. "Peer Tutoring: A Contradiction in Terms?" *The Writing Center Journal* 7 (2): 21–28.

7

Sites for (Invisible) Intellectual Work

Margaret J. Marshall

> The traditional representation of academic work as
> research, teaching, or service does not simply differentiate
> faculty activities in a neutral or objective way but also
> implicitly ranks them in order of esteem. . . . Without a dra-
> matic shift in perspective, it seems impossible to get away
> from the power and apparent inevitability of the model's
> assumptions and connotations, which have become so natu-
> ralized as to be invisible.
>
> (Modern Language Association Commission
> on Professional Service 1996, 169–70)

When the MLA formed the Commission on Professional Service to "examine the ways in which faculty work has been defined, evaluated, and rewarded" (161), it recognized the cultural and economic forces that have altered the roles of university faculty as well as the inadequacy of traditional models for representing and evaluating scholarship, teaching, and service. Indeed, when the commission defined its task, in part, as making visible the connections between teaching, scholarship, and service that otherwise would be invisible, necessitating a redefinition of these terms, it took an important step in reforming faculty rewards to better match the practices of higher education. The commission's final report adopts the language of "sites" in arguing that faculty work is more usefully evaluated in terms of its intellectual dimensions and coherence across numerous sites, including those more typically thought of as "service," like writing centers.

To those who work in writing centers, it is no revelation that such locations are sites for intellectual projects involving literacy, discourse practices, teacher education, and institutional policy, to name but a few of the possibilities. The difficulty has been making this work visible to those who have no intimate contact with writing centers and who assume that what goes on there is limited to individualized teaching of basic language skills. As the Council of Writing Program Administrators' statement on "Evaluating the Intellectual Work of Writing Administration" (1998) points out, administration, particularly administration associated with writing, has been treated "as a management activity that does not produce new knowledge and that neither requires nor demonstrates scholarly expertise and disciplinary knowledge" (85). Such a view must have been at work when the MLA Commission placed writing centers halfway between intellectual work and service on their chart of faculty work. Of course, such prepositioning denies the contextual differences of individual institutions and careers that ought to be considered in evaluating the intellectual contribution of a particular individual's work at any site; it would be just as inaccurate to assume that every publication breaks new intellectual ground or that every act of teaching demonstrates the highest standards of intellectual engagement and critical reflection.

My interest in this essay is not to criticize the MLA Commission but to describe the difficulties inherent in arguing that writing centers be treated as sites for intellectual work. While I believe it is possible to argue that tutoring in a writing center is intellectual work, it is the work of directing a writing center that usually causes more difficulty because of the time it requires, its apparent disconnection from either research or teaching, and directors' need to establish the framework within which their work is evaluated. This essay will describe three interconnected challenges inherent in making the argument that directing a writing center is, indeed, intellectual work. First, the activities that go on in writing centers must be documented in order to make them visible. Second, once documented, the work must be evaluated using criteria very similar to that employed in evaluating other features of faculty labor. Third, even if documented and evaluated appropriately within the field of composition, explicit and hidden institutional practices can still recast the work of writing centers as bureaucratic management detached from the intellectual interests of faculty, or as invisible "service." It is this last challenge that is the most insidious, the most difficult to fight, and the least likely to be overcome by individuals connected to writing centers or acting within the boundaries of specific institutions.

Documenting the Work of Writing Centers

Directing a writing center, even a well-established writing center, is difficult and time-consuming work. Directors regularly monitor peer tutors, direct internships, meet with students to hear complaints, answer queries, and frequently do a share of tutoring as well. They attend meetings to reconsider undergraduate curriculum, alter programs for incoming students, expand the opportunities for foreign students, or enhance the writing-across-the-curriculum (WAC) offerings. They meet with individual faculty to answer questions about services, strategize about how best to help particular students, and offer advice about designing assignments, responding to student writing, or proposing new writing courses. They conduct faculty workshops, train and supervise tutors, and resolve, mediate, and negotiate the numerous conflicts that inevitably arise over limited space, inadequate funds, and competing agendas.

Given such people-centered activities, it is no small task to create written documents that make the work of the writing center visible to those who aren't a regular part of its life. But to argue that the conception of writing centers be transformed from "service" to "sites for intellectual projects," documents must be created to articulate, track, and evaluate the work going on in these sites. Directors can, of course, write up their work for publication and thereby transform it into the category of "research," but even when they are able to get their work into print, the journals and presses that publish such pieces are frequently assigned less prestige. Furthermore, because of the content, these publications are likely to be devalued or dismissed as "merely" pedagogical scholarship. Besides, much of what writing-center directors do is local, necessarily part of an ongoing plan for institutional change, or otherwise unsuitable for widespread dissemination. The larger problem, though, is that offering "research" publications as the only evidence of writing-center work does not really reconceptualize the sites for intellectual projects or force the reevaluation of nontraditional materials as evidence of intellectual work; insisting that writing-center work be published reinforces the expectations for something that looks like traditional scholarship even if the topic is nontraditional.

If the goal is to find a way to evaluate the intellectual dimensions of work in writing centers and not dismiss that work as "service," then evaluation ought to be based on written documents that writing centers routinely produce, and directors need to find ways to create documents that serve the purposes of the writing center even as they also make the work that goes on there more visible. For example, directors can write end-of-year reports describing the major projects undertaken, the statistics of student usage, and the plans for the following year. Many writing centers compose or revise mission statements, put oral traditions into the written form of policy manuals, or create tutoring handbooks for new staff members. Proposals for additional funds or new ventures; materials from peer-tutoring programs; observation letters for individual writing-center consultants; letters to faculty members describing the support available from the writing center; materials created for staff meetings, workshops, or presentations; reports on individual student writers or student tutors; website materials and online tutorials; handouts created for students or faculty—these documents are part of the routine business of writing centers and their directors but are frequently overlooked when the time comes to evaluate that work.

Creating such documents as a part of the daily work of the writing center is actually less difficult than offering such documents for evaluation; faculty members are regularly required to turn in reports for merit pay, but the standard forms rarely ask for documentation of administrative work like directing a writing center. Even if directors find ways of creating, collecting, and offering documents of their work, they will encounter a second problem: since the documents are created for other purposes, it is difficult for nonexperts to read them as signs of an ongoing intellectual project. Often a document like an end-of-year report is accomplishing several goals simultaneously, and the portion that speaks to the specific intellectual agenda of the director may not be foregrounded any more than a syllabus for a particular class would foreground the connections to the instructor's research.

Suppose, for example, that a director's career is centered on WAC. She uses the writing center to advance her intellectual project of understanding writing from various disciplinary perspectives, beginning a series of discussions with faculty from other departments about the connections they could forge with and through the writing center. Documents that demonstrate how the writing center is a contribution to that project of understanding and creating new knowledge about WAC ought to be useful to those who wish to evaluate the intellectual contribution of the director, but will a series of notes from meetings with individual faculty be recognized as the first step in such knowledge making? Will the creation of workshop material for new faculty be understood as requiring the same kind of extensive preparation as a graduate seminar? Will a proposal to fund graduate students in non-English departments to work in the writing center be accepted as the product of expertise and innovation? If the evaluation of the director's work is happening within an English department, will the proposal to fund non-English department TA lines in the writing center be read as an intellectual dispute or as simply a "bad idea"?

As difficult as it is to get colleagues and an administration to understand the intellectual dimensions represented in the documents of teaching, it is even more difficult to get writing-center documents to be treated as evidence of serious, intellectual productivity. Sympathetic colleagues may be impressed by the amount of work being done, but their goodwill does not necessarily enable them to articulate the expertise that is involved or the degree of innovation or analysis being employed. Thus, a director may well have to write yet another document to frame the evidence offered for evaluation, and these documents too will be seen as unusual offerings; they can be misread as overkill, unnecessary attention to "service" when no one doubts the adequacy of this work. For faculty members who are also expected to produce more traditional scholarly publications, the extra attention given to the work of the writing center can draw suspicion to the other sites of faculty work. Evaluators may well reason that a director *could* be an even more productive scholar if only less time went toward writing center "service." What criteria, then, can be used to evaluate the documents of administration so that directors can be certain that their work will not be dismissed as "unreadable," counterproductive, or meaningless?

Evaluating Administration as Intellectual Work

The Council of Writing Program Administrators (1998) has developed a policy statement about "Evaluating the Intellectual Work of Writing Administration" that applies quite readily to directing a writing center. The document identifies five categories of intellectual work that apply to work in writing programs: program creation, curricular design, faculty development, program assessment and evaluation, and program-related textual production. In each of these categories, however, work would be considered "intellectual" only if it met one or more of four criteria:

1. It generates, clarifies, connects, reinterprets, or applies knowledge based on research, theory, and sound pedagogical practice.

2. It requires disciplinary knowledge available only to an expert trained in or conversant with a particular field.

3. It requires highly developed analytical or problem-solving skills derived from specific expertise, training, or research derived from scholarly knowledge.

4. It results in products or activities that can be evaluated by peers (e.g., publication, internal or outside evaluation, participant responses) as the contribution of the individual's insight, research, and disciplinary knowledge. (100)

Clearly, in order for work to be evaluated, there would have to be a portfolio of materials to represent the categories and the degrees to which the individual's activities met "more specific" criteria: innovation, improvement/refinement, dissemination, or empirical results (100).

The WPA is concerned with more general writing-program administration, but it is not difficult to see how these categories and criteria of evaluation could apply to a writing-center director as well. Even when a writing center has been in existence for some time, it is not unusual for a new director to be asked to develop and expand the activities of the center.

For example, despite the uninformed image of writing centers as primarily remedial support for the most marginal students, or fix-it shops for students who have numerous grammatical or mechanical errors, few writing centers limit their services in such ways. Writing-center personnel are usually quite aware of the demands of different discourses, of the uses of computer technology to support writing instruction, of learning differences, and of the cultural and language differences of nonnative speakers of English. Some writing centers are responsible for writing assessment of incoming students, for leading the development and teaching of writing-intensive courses, and for evaluating institutional initiatives connected to writing. Because of such knowledge and experience, writing centers often serve as an initial introduction to teaching, and some programs actually assign new teaching assistants to work as tutors in the writing center before having them assume full responsibility for a composition course; thus, writing-center directors are often very knowledgeable about teaching teachers and about research in writing pedagogy. Because writing doesn't stop once students leave the university, and because of the increased interest in putting students into real-world settings, writing centers are also logical sites for connecting the university to the community, so directors must understand nonacademic writing practices, service-learning programs, and institutional missions. Naturally, all these different aspects of writing-center work make writing centers a prime location for conducting studies of various kinds.

Some institutions may assign faculty to "direct" the writing center and expect something akin to a committee assignment—intervene in a crisis but otherwise leave the day-to-day work to the staff of graduate students and part-time faculty. Such an appointment ought rightly to be considered "service," and I am not arguing that every writing-center director should be treated the same. Indeed, the point is that since directors function differently, their work ought to be evaluated in ways that are most appropriate to their individual career profiles. Indeed, many institutions expect the director to be a leader in establishing and overseeing these multiple programs to support the culture of writing instruction on and off campus. To the degree that directors have to create these programs, design curriculum to fit various needs, support faculty efforts to teach writing more effectively, devise or execute ways to assess and evaluate student writing or the various writing programs, and produce documents related to these multiple efforts, they are clearly involved in one or more of the five categories identified by the WPA as signs of intellectual work. And with each effort, it ought to be possible to evaluate the degree and quality of that intellectual work using the criteria offered by the WPA.

Unfortunately, when directing a writing center is recognized as a major responsibility, it is often constructed as a purely administrative task detached from tenure-line faculty appointments. Dave Healy's 1995 survey of writing-center directors reported that only 46 percent of the directors were tenure-track faculty (30). Sometimes these appointments are advertised as limited contracts, suitable for those without a doctorate, or for those with limited publications and/or little interest in traditional research. Such institutional arrangements can be to the director's benefit if they protect the individual director from the politics of traditional English departments or the turf wars raging within an institution. Direct access to the provost or president of the institution can also be a benefit to the director and to the writing center, and those institutions with unionized faculty are sometimes constrained by the collective bargaining agreement so that an appointment must be either faculty or administration but not both. In other words, there may be very good reasons for an institution to categorize the writing-center director as an administrator and not as a faculty member. But just as often, the unexamined and unspoken message is that directing a writing center might require special interest and special expertise, but not the interest or expertise associated with "faculty" work, not, that is, intellectual work but institutional and bureaucratic labor. Individuals applying for the position or agreeing to assume these responsibilities are rarely able to argue for a reconfiguration of the job to match their ideal view of the position. If they are fortunate enough to find institutional support for treating it as both a faculty and administrative position, the criteria for tenure as a faculty member are not likely to include evaluation of the nontraditional intellectual work of the administrative position. Instead, such a position may provide release time from teaching for the administration work, pay the director on a twelve-month contract rather than a typical faculty nine- or ten-month appointment, or offer other compensation for the "work" of administering the center; scholarship, teaching, and service in the form of departmental committees or good citizenship will still be expected in order to qualify for tenure or promotion.

Of course, even an administrative position ought to have a job description and criteria for evaluation, and embedded in each of these is a conception of the features of intellectual work. Thus, it behooves all writing centers to be certain that the conception underlying these positions is appropriate, and that the criteria and job description are consistent with the best understanding of the intellectual demands of the position, even if the formal designation cannot recognize the hybrid nature of administration as intellectual work.

Rendered Invisible and Recast as Service

Healy's survey (1995) reported that only 40 percent of directors or assistant directors had Ph.D.s and only 10 percent identified their field of expertise as composition/rhetoric, so perhaps it isn't surprising that writing centers aren't widely conceived as sites for intellectual work; after all, how could directors expect their work to be evaluated with the criteria established by the WPA if the appointment itself doesn't "require disciplinary knowledge available only to an expert trained in or conversant with a particular field"? Perhaps the assumption is that all graduate programs provide enough study in composition and teaching to adequately prepare writing-center directors to be "conversant in the field." More likely, I suspect, the preconception of writing-center work as "service" allows institutions to hire directors willing to assume the responsibilities and then ignore the difficulties of evaluating their work.

Even for the few faculty who undertake directing a writing center because they see it as a site for advancing their intellectual projects, the structure of institutional review regularly precludes submission of the very documents that would demonstrate the intellectual dimensions of directing a writing center. Where institutions encourage a full submission of the documents of faculty work, writing-center documents are likely to be classified as either "service" or "teaching," and both categories can be treated seriously without giving attention to the criteria outlined by the WPA. In other words, directing a writing center can be seen, like teaching, as important work but different from—and ultimately probably less important than—scholarly publications.

Because the usual procedures of review for tenure or promotion ask that the candidate submit publications separately from teaching or service, because colleagues on review committees have no more time than other faculty for reading detailed documents or superfluous evidence, because deans have developed routines that do not get modified in the face of the unusual profile of the faculty writing-center director, because even those faculty producing these "other" documents would not think to call them "publications," the work of directing a writing center remains in a very literal sense invisible. An end-of-year report on writing-center activities might or might not be referred to by others who speak on a director's behalf, but it will certainly not be listed as a "publication," and so colleagues across the university may never realize the amount of intellectual work, the significant time and writing skill, or the creativity required to imagine a new form for representing lived events that such reports require. Likewise, an assessment of curriculum that involves the writing center requires considerable time and expertise but is likely to result in a report meant for internal circulation and does not figure in the category of "scholarly production." Colleagues not associated with writing centers cannot be expected to evaluate these materials as they might evaluate an article or a contribution to a collection of essays if the materials themselves are not put forward as such. And because few who would identify their primary field as composition/rhetoric and who direct writing centers have made their way into the hierarchies of administration and senior faculty, there are few localities with insider advocates to argue for changing the procedures, to pave the way, or to pass on the secrets of the process.

More disturbing still, given the heavily gendered nature of writing instruction (Barr-Ebest 1995), is that even the strongest feminist allies sometimes balk at the argument that administration is intellectual work. Since Healy (1995) reports that 74 percent of writing-center directors are female, the difficulty of making the work visible and insisting that it be evaluated as a part of an intellectual product is imbricated with the already gendered assumptions about "nurturing," and thus with assumptions about the anti-intellectual activities of writing centers. Likewise, writing-center directors cannot escape the class-based elitism of those who object to open admissions, or who assume that writing centers serve only remedial students. Even if the class and race issues imbedded in these assumptions remain hidden, the prejudice inherent in such views is quite visible in the reluctance of most faculty to join the tutorial staff for a portion of their teaching load, or to evaluate the contributions of writing-center directors as they would other intellectual projects.

As the MLA's Commission on Professional Service (1996) pointed out, some of what faculty members do is more a product of their citizenship in the department, institution, or profession than a result of an intellectual project, and it is certainly possible to direct a writing center as a "service" to a department or an institution. But for those who take on writing-center work because they believe it is a site for their intellectual projects, the current structural practices do a great injustice. Written tenure guidelines might suggest that the teaching and administrative materials collected and offered up for evaluation will be considered, but unwritten are the "normal" practices that do not provide faculty review committees with copies of all these documents, nor require that the committee members examine the full portfolio before passing judgment. It is thus essential that writing-center documents be included in the materials sent to outside reviewers and that those reviewers assess the degree and quality of intellectual work inherent in such materials just as they assess the quality of more traditional forms of scholarship. Likewise, departmental tenure committees and chairs who write representations of the faculty director's work have an obligation to describe these documents as part of the director's ongoing intellectual project. Even when the director's position is constructed as an administrative position, the evaluation ought to recognize and reward the intellectual dimensions of the work so as to make the connections to expertise, knowledge building, and peer review visible to faculty and other administrators.

Only with such evaluative practices in place and rigorously defended can writing-center directors expect to transport their intellectual projects to other institutions without having their contributions recast as merely institutional service. Furthermore, if writing centers are to be kept viable as sites for intellectual work, they need the regular influx of composition scholars with intellectual projects centered on such diverse issues as teacher education, disciplinary writing practices, community literacy, rhetorical history, discourse communities, narrative arguments, basic writing, nonstandard English, orality, or institutional policies. Such a variety of interests will keep writing centers on the forefront of composition studies and allow writing-center directors to connect their intellectual projects to the administration of the center, even if they do so for only a limited time before returning to full-time faculty roles or other administrative positions like directing a writing program. An assignment to direct a writing center could be a particularly enriching site for faculty to work with writers, teachers, disciplinary issues, and institutional priorities that they might otherwise never encounter. But what faculty member can afford to take on these responsibilities without the assurance that the work will be valued and evaluated in keeping with their other intellectual projects?

It seems fairly clear, then, that no matter how hard an individual director works to create documents to represent the invisible work of a writing center, no matter how carefully such documents are evaluated by individuals who are sympathetic to the view that writing centers are sites for intellectual work, various institutional habits can still recast these contributions as "service" and thereby render their intellectual dimensions invisible and ignorable. Such a tripartite division of faculty efforts, a senior faculty member recently pointed out to me, "may be wrong, but it's been in existence since the middle ages." If her admonition was meant to engender greater respect for traditions, I'm afraid it failed miserably in my case, but it did give me a better understanding of the difficulty of making the argument I'm making here to the senior colleagues who must evaluate work for tenure and promotion. Changing habits of mind and the unexamined assumptions at work in evaluating writing centers and the work of their directors is an effort that requires the collective energies of those associated with writing centers, including those faculty and administrators who serve on search committees and prepare graduate students for positions in higher education. Writing-center professionals can begin, I think, by monitoring their own tendencies to talk about teaching, scholarship, and administrative service as separate categories and instead insist on describing the multiple sites of their intellectual projects.

Works Cited

Barr-Ebest, S. 1995. "Gender Differences in Writing Program Administration." *WPA: Writing Program Administration* 18 (3): 53–73.

Council of Writing Program Administrators. 1998. "Evaluating the Intellectual Work of Writing Administration." *WPA: Writing Program Administration* 22 (1/2): 85–104.

Healy, D. 1995. "Writing Center Directors: An Emerging Portrait of the Profession." *WPA: Writing Program Administration* 18 (3): 26–43.

Modern Language Association Commission on Professional Service. 1996. "Making Faculty Work Visible: Reinterpreting Professional Service, Teaching, and Research in the Fields of Language and Literature." In *Profession 1996*, 161–216. New York: MLA.

8

The Politics of Administrative and Physical Location

Carol Peterson Haviland, Carmen M. Fye, and Richard Colby

Much of writing-center directors' considerable energies become caught up in selecting and educating tutors, engaging with faculty members, taking writing-across-the-curriculum (WAC) workshops to classrooms, conducting research, negotiating budgets, and tutoring face-to-face and online. Believing that what writing centers do is more important than where they are located or how reporting lines are drawn, it is easy for directors simply to make the best of whatever space and administrative structures they are offered. And, to a degree, this priority is correct; neither style nor location is a good substitute for substance. However, although location is not everything, it too is important, for material spaces have political edges that are costly if ignored. Location is political because it is an organizational choice that creates visibility or invisibility, access to resources, and associations that define the meanings, uses, and users of designated spaces.

In "Composition's Imagined Geographies: The Politics of Space in the Frontier, City, and Cyberspace" (1998), Nedra Reynolds cites Edward Soja on the politics of space as she affirms that *where* writing instruction takes place has everything to do with *how*: "We must be insistently aware of how space can be made to hide consequences from us, how relations of power and discipline are inscribed into the apparently innocent spatiality of social life, how human geographies become filled with politics and ideology" (Soja 1989, 6). Just as CEOs know that spacious offices with panoramic views radiate status, and their vice presidents compete for proximity to presidents' offices, writing-center directors should recognize that their physical and administrative locations contribute substantively to the roles that they play on their campuses. These locations, Reynolds reminds us, shape the roles others perceive writing, writers, and writing centers to play as well as the images writers and writing centers have of themselves. Thus, the spaces that writing centers occupy and the reporting lines that are drawn have real implications for the politics of location.

A review of writing-center texts and two active listservs (WCenter and WPA) reveals a wide range of possible locations: some are free-standing, independent programs reporting to chief academic officers, while others are within or attached to a variety of academic centers and departments, such as general studies, humanities or arts and letters, WAC, English, composition, freshman writing, creative writing, foreign language, media centers, or libraries. Still others are part of or adjacent to student-service programs, such as teaching-resource centers, learning centers, student unions, residence halls, women's resource centers, multicultural centers, international student or ESL programs, services to students with disabilities, economic-opportunity programs, or athletic programs; and still others are located simply wherever there's space. Finally, increasing portions of writing centers are located in cyberspace, a place with even more complicated meanings. In this chapter, we examine the multiple and competing agendas of students, tutors, staff/faculty members, and administrators as campuses locate their writing centers, identifying the questions and possibilities that can sketch the political terrain of writing-center location.

Writing-Center Locations

The meaning of writing on any campus is contested and thus presents a significant location consideration. Viewing writing as simply eradicating errors that students shouldn't be making in the first place makes one political statement: student writing is an unfortunate problem that administrators and faculty wish they didn't have to solve so they create writing centers to fix it as quickly and cheaply as possible, preferably out of sight. Viewing writing as more than English department–defined correctness and as central to cross-disciplinary intellectual activity makes quite a different political statement: writing is central to learning, working on writing need not be hidden, and writing centers are hubs of multidisciplinary scholarly activity. However, even though this latter statement stakes out significant political territory for writing, it does not resolve all of the competing possibilities.

Elizabeth Boquet (1999) contrasts these possibilities as the "method" and "site" definitions for writing centers. Drawing on what Nancy Grimm (1996) calls a "regulatory" writing-center model, Boquet describes the method center "as producing and sustaining hegemonic institutional discourses" (466). These centers often become institutional insiders as they stabilize norms rather than challenge them, which may net them administrators' favor. In contrast, locating writing centers as sites, as part of the extracurriculum, sets "the precedent for a counter-hegemonic model of writing center operations, one which attempts to wrest authority out of the hands of the institution and place it in the hands of the students" (466). When centers recognize what Grimm (1996) asserts are "the cultural conflicts embedded in literacy" (530), they embrace education's ostensible goals of intellectual curiosity and discovery, which include challenging norms, a stance that administrators often publicly salute. Yet encouraging writing centers in their liberatory roles is risky for administrators, for they can manage only a certain amount of challenge or disequilibrium without risking their own positions. Thus, they may hobble border or outlaw writing centers that encourage students to problematize writing assignments and challenge the norms of academic discourse by locating them away from influence, money, windows, and custodial services. Having your cake and eating it too remains difficult. Clearly, the arguments for both philosophical and physical location problematize the relationships writing centers may have with their sponsors and their users—and they remind us once again of the tangle postmodernism creates. Recognizing that even the most careful thinking about which meanings of writing that writing centers wish to enact cannot produce single, stable answers, we now turn to weighing the political implications of some specific locations.

Freestanding Writing Centers

Freestanding centers may enjoy the greatest autonomy and access to resources if they are viewed favorably and have short reporting lines. For example, highly respected centers that report directly to a chief academic officer rely less on middle management to broker their policy decisions or space and budget requests. Very simply, directors who rarely see the vice presidents who shape policies and distribute money may find their contributions and needs disregarded. As Jeanne Simpson (1997), a director turned administrator, puts it,

> the closer to the funding source, the better off a center will be. . . . The logic of the argument is easy. Every layer of authority siphons off more money. And every layer of authority is a place where a request can be vetoed or just ignored or reordered among priorities. The fewer layers, the fewer opportunities to be told no, and the fewer opportunities for a budget to be trimmed. . . . A department may be very supportive in terms of sending people to the center, in terms of sharing the

workload, in terms of feeling good about the center, in terms of supporting the director's efforts toward tenure and promotion. But department faculty don't sign the checks and they don't approve the budgets.

Writing-center director Donna Dunbar-Odom (1997) echoes Simpson's observations: make "your connection with the highest (most
powerful) administrative entity possible." However, Ed Lotto (1997)
cautions that "it is important to keep writing centers in the academic
side of the university both for credibility and to make sure some
nonacademic administrator doesn't get a bright idea for what we can
do that will destroy the sound pedagogical underpinnings of the place."
Thus, this access may come at a cost. Greater visibility may result in
greater indebtedness and control, and administrative ties may create
faculty and student wariness. In addition, directors so located may feel
isolated, particularly from discipline-based scholarship. Affiliation has
political consequences, and in this case it may mean compromising
academic collegiality and gadfly status for insider access.

Writing Centers Located Within or Attached to Academic Departments or Centers

Those who argue for physical and reporting links with academic
departments or centers note that these are the heart of any university,
describing administrative and student-service programs as necessary
but peripheral to the important work of education—classroom teaching
and research. English departments, for example, point to the importance of composition studies as an undergirding theoretical base, one
that grows chiefly out of rhetoric and composition, which is a closer
cousin to English than to any other discipline. But locating in English
departments does not guarantee freedom and resources to shape writing centers with that scholarship. Lotto (1997) notes that he likes "to
stay out of the English department because they often have different
ideas about what it means to teach writing and I like the independence
that allows me to argue forcefully for my sense of good writing pedagogy." Also, unless writing centers develop their own strong identities,
they run the same risks of occupying departmental stepsister or hand-
maiden positions that they encounter within any hierarchical structure.
Other academic department locations may include a variety of writing
programs, linguistics, communications studies, and foreign languages,
each linking writing centers with traditional academic missions and
thus carrying a kind of legitimacy both for the work the centers do and
for the staff who do it. Such locations also offer clearer tenure possibilities for staff, which Joanne Cavallaro (1994c) maintains is essential: "I seem to need it [tenure], at least in this context. I have been

stymied over and over because I don't have it or because our [department] is not part of the academic program." Tom Denton (1994), however, cautions that if directors are tenured, it should be in an academic department and not as a writing-center director, a choice that could sacrifice "vision and energy" to "stability and complacency."

In addition, academic centers such as general or undergraduate studies, arts and letters, WAC, or libraries offer logical writing-center connections. Those who argue for cohabitation with academic centers outside of single departments show how WAC programs (Haviland 1985) and other interdisciplinary academic centers, such as teaching and learning or teaching excellence centers (Nelson 1994a), enact the interdisciplinary nature of writing and thus its role as crossing rather than maintaining traditional disciplinary boundaries. Indeed, linking writing centers to WAC programs often sweeps aside the cloak of remediation. Richard Jenseth (1999) characterizes a writing center of this kind as an activity, not a place, "something that people (faculty, tutors, students, director) DO." The Writing Program Administrators (WPA) listserv moderator David Schwalm (1999b) agrees that writing centers are central players in much larger interdisciplinary designs for teaching composition as well as traditionally discipline-confined courses. Defining writing's roles with these broad strokes points to locations that enact intersections rather than single departmental locations. Thus, as Howard Tinberg (1999) says, "We have faculty working in the writing lab representing all academic divisions within the college." Jenseth (1999) elaborates, "The more faculty and [departments] you can get involved and invested, the better."

Several responses to WCenter listserv queries on location suggest that library space is most compatible with writing centers' objectives. Jane Nelson (1994b), for example, says, "We have our own space, a very pleasant room with walls, a door, a couple of smaller offices inside . . . I'm delighted to be in the library. The Writing Center is part of a large center, the Center for Teaching Excellence, and the whole center has beautiful space." However, her comment includes an important proviso—"our own space"—that other not-so-delighted library-located directors describe. John Edlund (1994b), for example, warns that library space often is very different from writing space, particularly in tolerance of noise and disruption, and that librarians, like many other landowners, can be territorial and treat writing centers like tenants rather than neighbors.

Writing centers can more easily enact rich definitions of writing if they are located outside of single academic departments, particularly English departments, but these outside locations can separate students, isolate directors, and frustrate administrators. Even as cross-disciplinary locations reinforce a cross-disciplinary role for writing, they create other difficulties. The more fragmented programs become, the less control any director can exert over them. And widely scattered locations that are philosophically desirable can be physically inconvenient. Linda Bergmann (1999) reminds us that locating writing centers outside of English departments more fully defines writing but also means "a lot of running across campus, since it is also crucial for me to keep an office and an intellectual presence in the English department."

Writing Centers and Student-Services Centers

High-traffic crossroads, such as student unions or libraries, are most appropriate, contends Diana Roloff (1998), aligning writing with other advising, counseling, learning, adult reentry, women's and multicultural centers, or other student-support services. Combining writing and learning centers has evoked the most vigorous debate on both listserv threads. Some directors point to shared philosophy and resources while others warn against philosophical differences and the remediation stigma. Proponents of this space sharing point to the ways learning centers "work with the whole student, not just her writing" (Cavallaro 1994a), so tutors can come together to address a wider range of learning issues. Cavallaro (1994b) also argues that student affairs deans are more willing to provide financial support because support services are what they do as opposed to what they wish they didn't have to do. Anne Mullin (1994) agrees, observing that not only does the student services collegiality benefit students, but also "funding and facilities are definitely more favorable for us than if we were a nodule on the English Department branch."

Daphne Bryan and Bob Holderer counter this optimism, pointing to several problems. Bryan (1999) notes that because high schools use the label Learning Center "almost exclusively . . . to refer specifically to facilities for students with learning disabilities . . . some of our students do not use the [university] Writing Center because they do not want to be labeled as a student with a disability." While Holderer (1994a) worries about the remediation image and competition with learning-center tutors who want to deal with writing themselves, he also suggests that "writing centers can become part of larger learning centers and keep their integrity . . . [if] the head of the writing center becomes head of the learning skills center or . . . has a great deal of autonomy" (1994b). This certainly tugs at power relationships, and it also nudges writing-center directors to be willing to help others redefine themselves just as they have asked for that same help. As Eric Crump (1994) observes, "I don't think it helps our cause much to simply deposit the label [remedial] on somebody else." Indeed, defining remediation as distasteful work conflicts with writing centers' theoretical commitment to diverse communities of learners.

Nelson (1994a) describes an interesting bridge between English department and student-service locations—a Center for Teaching Excellence—particularly because it also houses the campus WAC program. This center supports the university's teaching mission, sponsors competitive grants for travel and curriculum innovation, offers seminars and colloquia for faculty and TAs, and provides individual consulting. In addition to the writing center and WAC, the center houses the instructional computing and media centers. Nelson's model is attractive in that rather than try to escape the remedial function, it simply defines itself within a faculty context—which faculty members are unlikely to label remedial—and then makes the writing connection between faculty members and their students. And here, as Nelson (1998) reminds us, writing centers' liminal or "in the middle" positions are an asset:

> The central [physical] location . . . has allowed us to do many things we could never have done otherwise. Perhaps most important, the collegiality of several people working outside of the traditional department structure has resulted in many innovative and productive programs . . . the central location acts as a catalyst for making temporary and sometimes permanent associations with all kinds of programs that do not literally move to "our" space—but the combining of resources this way yields even more productive programs.

Indeed, Boquet (1999) celebrates just this space, the coming together of site and method: "the writing center is most interesting to me for its post-disciplinary possibilities, for the contradictions it embraces, for its tendency to go off-task" (478).

Multiple Rather Than Single Locations

Of course, all campus units compete for the ideal geographic spot—convenient to parking, major classrooms, libraries and laboratories, and food—and access issues are more complicated the larger an institution's size. However, regardless of campus size, the principle of geographic convenience for students might prescribe multiple discipline-based writing centers so that chemistry majors could use writing labs based in the natural science complex where they take most of their classes, and accounting majors could stay in the school of business and management without having to trek across campus and encounter unfamiliar territory. General college or undeclared majors could work in a central undergraduate college location. In addition, other satellite centers might be located in residence halls, athletic centers, and student unions. In fact, Michelle Eodice (1998) describes a six-location configuration that relies on cell phone communication and tutors who carry "a tutoring-in-a-box kit which includes reference books, the cell phone, database forms, and campus referral guide. We developed portable signs with our logo so we could set up quickly in our locations, put out the sign, and get down to it." Certainly, these multiple locations would offer convenient access to students on large campuses, and such arrangements would respond to students' complaints that they just can't "get over to the writing center." In addition, they could make writing and writing centers more visible by permeating multiple scenes and expanding campuses' definitions of literacy.

However, spreading out writing centers for geographic and disciplinary convenience may also conflict with the strands of composition theory that draw on interdisciplinary collaboration and ignore the politics of campus material spaces (Reynolds 1998, 30). This practice could make it even less likely that theatre majors will ever see physics majors after their sophomore years, and it could reinforce the separation of rhetoric and ideas, eroding richer definitions of writing and confining writing to composition instruction within English departments. Thus, the practice has the potential to cement both students' and faculty members' impressions that chemists and historians have little in common and that universities are joined properly by very long sidewalks, not by thinking or questions. Sometimes, thus, locations such as libraries, student-learning centers, or faculty-teaching centers can even more readily enact these interdisciplinary meanings of writing.

Writing-center directors insert another set of convenience dilemmas—this time for their own physical and professional concerns. Writing centers located away from English or composition departments support the interdisciplinary nature of writing. However, not only may they involve a great deal of walking, particularly on large campuses, they also may isolate directors from the conversation and disciplinary resources they need to flourish. On the one hand, they see writing as central to learning in all disciplines, but on the other hand, they most often feel at home in English or composition departments, a conflict even more complicated by questions of faculty/staff/tenure considerations. To possible charges that directors may serve themselves at the expense of students, Schwalm (1999a) comments,

> There is no reason on earth why education must be totally student centered. Faculty need to derive some satisfaction from the process too. Actually, everyone in an academic community—students, faculty, staff, vice provosts—should find opportunities for self-realization and positive professional identity. The shift to a heavier concentration on learning—as done by our students, not as we remember ourselves

learning—demands a rebuilding (not just a tweaking) of the institution, with new paths to new kinds of self-realization for all parties.

Administrators insert a different convenience concern: reporting lines. If writing centers are multiply located, they tend to involve more people and lengthier chains of command. Administrators, who already juggle meetings and staff, usually look to consolidate rather than diversify management slots. Despite the turn to interdisciplinarity, universities, like most structures, prefer to parcel work out tidily. For writing, this often means assigning responsibility to a single location—usually an English department, composition program, or writing center. If writing is thought of as a skill that one can pick up much like a crate of oranges, it then makes sense to locate it in a "writing space" just as oranges are located in a "food space." Students can go to the proper space, get the desired fix, and then return to the real business of education. However, administrators' preferences for tidy categories and short reporting lines may conflict with the interdisciplinary nature of writing and with directors' needs for access to those administrators.

Writing Centers Online: Trading Real Spaces for Virtual Ones

Virtual spaces are as complex as real spaces, as the debate over the egalitarian potential of e-spaces demonstrates. Some compositionists maintain that e-spaces are egalitarian because many electronic discussions take place without the face-to-face "paraphernalia that allow physical context to . . . inhibit the pure exchange of ideas" (Barker and Kemp 1990, 21). Therefore, what is said online is not superseded by who is saying it (Hawisher and Sullivan 1998, 174). However, others argue that these "paraphernalia" are important context for constructing social spaces and that e-spaces are better suited to simpler communicating of businesslike information (Hawisher and Sullivan, 174). Both perspectives are relevant to a discussion of location because the work writing centers do has such potential to create intimate and liminal spaces between tutors and students, particularly in face-to-face sessions. Egalitarian or not, the social and physical surroundings of tutoring sessions contribute significantly to the conversations that construct the sessions, whether in virtual or real settings.

Presently, the work of most online writing labs (OWLs) is located within already existing physical writing-center locations. For example, Lisa McClure (1998) describes a central communications-across-the-curriculum location that situates CAC, freshman composition, the writing center, and the technology and learning center under a single umbrella, each remaining "structurally related to the appropriate administrative unit (Writing Studies and the Writing Center to the Department of English and CAC and Technology and Learning to the Vice Chancellor of Academic Affairs)." One might assume that such OWLs are shaped by the same pedagogical and political elements as their hosts because tech-newbie writing-center tutors and directors design and maintain OWLs, perpetuating many of the familiar face-to-face practices.

Nonetheless, these assumptions are quickly shattered as OWL designers and users see conflicts. For example, technology can create a kind of distancing that is less common in face-to-face conferences. Online tutoring also offers even greater possibilities for misinterpretation, even when conferences are synchronous and use audio, video, and written communication. OWL access is an even more contested issue in moves toward cyberspace (Reynolds 1998, 28). Although more and more people are gaining access to computers and the Internet, a sizable number still have neither the access to nor facility with this technology. Online writing centers, no matter how egalitarian in structure, still deny participation to the disenfranchised and thus exacerbate rather than diminish access issues.

Although OWL designs draw on their history in face-to-face conferences as well as their bases in physical spaces, they need not be trapped by these designs, for virtual spaces can be attractive and constructive for potential users. Particularly on commuter campuses, OWLs can meet students' needs to conduct conferences at work, at home, or during off-hours. Also, they may provide the anonymity that some students prefer, and they may show apprehensive writers how easily they can communicate with another—in writing—when speech is not available. In addition, administrators may find technology attractive for another reason. As Ray Wallace (1998) states, "Writing center requests [for technology] were generally agreed to by higher administrators eager to show they could make 'cutting edge' decisions" (164).

However, the political implications of these "cutting edge" decisions are significant when enlightened decisions morph into frightening ones. For example, administrators under pressure to service as many students as possible with limited resources may assume that the virtual spaces of a computer network such as the Internet are a great deal cheaper and more efficient than the brick and mortar that presently house sites of literacy, and they may see tutors as less free to "color outside of the lines" online. These omens of schools of the future, in which computers replace tutors and even more faculty work is pieced out, evoke Freire's (1970) warning: "The more completely the majority adapt to the purposes which the dominant minority prescribe for them (thereby depriving them of the right to their own purposes), the more easily the minority can continue to prescribe" (63). Indeed, if writing centers are constructed solely in cyberspace with fewer humans tutoring, they have the potential to grow further from universities' human faces. The possibility of the Orwellian future that Tuman (1992, 9) fears, one that hides workers in a vast ether panopticon, well lit and watchfully monitored, reminds us yet again that location is political and that it matters.

Making Political Choices

As *The Writing Center Journal* coeditor Joan Mullin asserts in almost every discussion of writing centers, context matters. Just as the listserv responses demonstrate that colleagues can problematize but not answer the question of where a specific center should be located, this chapter cannot chart fixed answers. It does, however, pose some central questions that can shape answers, and it closes by highlighting four central political elements.

1. Location docs not "just happen." Space and its assignments are political, and the roles writing and writers play both shape and are shaped by writing-center locations. As Edlund (1994a) urges, "When they accuse you of being territorial you should say 'I believe in what I am doing and I need a space to do it in.'" He continues, "Whatever you do, don't just sit back and accept the situation" (1994b).

2. Proximity matters. Visibility and access to decision makers, resources, and users open or constrain possibilities. Paula Gillespie's (1998) complaint is important to heed: "We're housed now in a very bad location, far from everything." Visibility and access matter at the smaller scale, too. As Muriel Harris (1998) urges, "I'd vote for your desk in the writing center, not in an enclosed office . . . because I'm an advocate of being right in the middle of things, listening, talking, interacting, and always available to everyone."

3. People inhabit structures. Even the best theoretical structures may collapse when a prince or princess of a dean or vice president is replaced with a toad. Crump's (1994) warning is apt: "It matters a lot not only what the local administrative scheme is like, but who is running the thing."

4. Postmodern structures are not fixed. Even the most elegantly situated writing centers should be prepared to reshape and be reshaped. Indeed, many of the spaces we discuss will disappear as virtual spaces continue to increase, but the political implications of our choices will persist.

Works Cited

Barker, T. T., and F. O. Kemp. 1990. "Network Theory: A Postmodern Theory for the Writing Classroom." In *Computers and Community: Teaching Composition in the Twenty-First Century*, edited by C. Handa, 1–27. Portsmouth, NH: Boynton/Cook.

Bergmann, L. 1999. "Re: Writing Center Suggestions." Online posting. 21 January. In *Archives of WPA-L,* January 1999, no. 259 <http://lists.asu.edu/archives/wpa-l.html>.

Boquet, E. H. 1999. "'Our Little Secret': A History of Writing Centers, Pre- to Post-Open Admissions." *College Composition and Communication* 50 (3): 463–82.

Bryan, D. 1999. "Re: Politics of Location." Online posting. 4 February. In *WCENTER Archives* <http://www.ttu.edu/wcenter/9902/msg00112.html>.

Cavallaro, J. 1994a. "Re: Shared Location w/Learning Center." Online posting. 2 November. In *WCENTER Archives* <http://www.ttu.edu/wcenter/9411/msg00036.html>.

———. 1994b. "Re: Shared Location w/Learning Center." Online posting. 2 November. In *WCENTER Archives* <http://www.ttu.edu/wcenter/9411/msg00037.html>.

———. 1994c. "Re: Shared Location w/Learning Center." Online posting. 7 November. In *WCENTER Archives* <http://www.ttu.edu/wcenter/9411/msg00181.html>.

Crump, E. 1994. "Re: Re: Shared Location w/Learning Center." Online posting. 2 November. In *WCENTER Archives* <http://www.ttu.edu/wcenter/9411/msg00016.html>.

Denton, T. 1994. "Re: Re: Shared Location w/Learning Center." Online posting. 7 November. In *WCENTER Archives* <http://www.ttu.edu/wcenter/9411/msg00150.html>.

Dunbar-Odom, D. 1997. "Re: Writing Centers in English Depts. Or Academic Support." Online posting. 16 October. In *Archives of WPA-L,* October 1997, no. 300 <http://lists.asu.edu/archives/wpa-l.html>.

Edlund, J. R. 1994a. "Re: Justifying Space for WC to Admin. Types." Online posting. 9 September. In *WCENTER Archives* <http://www.ttu.edu/wcenter/9409/msg00074.html>.

———. 1994b. "Re: Justifying Space for WC to Admin. Types." Online posting. 10 September. In *WCENTER Archives* <http://www.ttu.edu/wcenter/9409/msg00082.html>.

Eodice, M. 1998. "Re: Location, Location: Residence Halls." Online posting. 4 December. In *WCENTER Archives* <http://www.ttu.edu/wcenter/9812/msg00138.html>.

Freire, P. [1970] 1988. *Pedagogy of the Oppressed.* New York: Continuum.

Gillespie, P. 1998. "Location, Location: Residence Halls." Online posting. 3

December. In *WCENTER Archives* <http://www.ttu.edu/wcenter/9812/msg00080.html>.

Grimm, N. M. 1996. "Rearticulating the Work of the Writing Center." *College Composition and Communication* 47 (4): 523–48.

Harris, M. 1998. "Re: Space Needs for New Writing Center." Online posting. 1 December. In *WCENTER Archives* <http://www.ttu.edu/wcenter/9812/msg00030.html>.

Haviland, C. P. 1985. "Writing Centers and Writing-Across-the-Curriculum: An Important Connection." *The Writing Center Journal* 5/6 (2/1): 25–30.

Hawisher, G. E., and P. Sullivan. 1998. "Women on the Networks: Searching for E-Spaces of Their Own." In *Feminism and Composition Studies: In Other Words*, edited by S. C. Jarratt and L. Worsham, 172–97. New York: MLA.

Holderer, B. 1994a. "Re: Re: Shared Location w/Learning Center." Online posting. 2 November. In *WCENTER Archives* <http://www.ttu.edu/wcenter/9411/msg00012.html>.

———. 1994b. "Re: Re: Shared Location w/Learning Center." Online posting. 4 November. In *WCENTER Archives* <http://www.ttu.edu/wcenter/9411/msg00118.html>.

Jenseth, R. 1999. "Re[2]: Writing Center Suggestions." Online posting. 20 January. In *Archives of WPA-l,* January 1999, no. 282 <http://lists.asu.edu/archives/wpa-l.html>.

Lotto, E. 1997. "Re: Writing Centers in English Depts. or Academic Support." Online posting. 16 October. In *Archives of WPA-L,* October 1997, no. 303 <http://lists.asu.edu/archives/wpa-l.html>.

McClure, L. J. 1998. "Greetings and Questions from C'dale." Online posting. 27 October. In *Archives of WPA-L,* October 1998, no. 176 <http://lists.asu.edu/archives/wpa-l.html>.

Mullin, A. E. 1994. "Re: Re: Shared Location w/Learning Center." Online posting. 4 November. In *WCENTER Archives* <http://www.ttu.edu/wcenter/9411/msg00114.html>.

Nelson, J. V. 1994a. "Re: Re: Shared Location w/Learning Center." Online posting. 2 November. In *WCENTER Archives* <http://www.ttu.edu/wcenter/9411/msg00033.html>.

———. 1994b. "Re: WCs as Communities." Online posting. 12 September. In *WCENTER Archives* <http://www.ttu.edu/wcenter/9409/msg00088.html>.

———. 1998. "Re: Greetings and Questions from C'dale." Online posting. 27 October. In *Archives of WPA-L,* October 1998, no. 174 <http://lists.asu.edu/archives/wpa-l.html>.

Reynolds, N. 1998. "Composition's Imagined Geographies: The Politics of Space in the Frontier, City, and Cyberspace." *College Composition and Communication* 50 (1): 12–35.

Roloff, D. L. 1998. "The Writing Center Environment." Unpublished essay.

Schwalm, D. 1999a. "Computer Classes/Swarming." Online posting. 15 January. In *Archives of WPA-L,* January 1999, no. 370 <http://lists.asu.edu/archives/wpa-l.html>.

———. 1999b. "Re: Computer Labs/Swarming/CM Classes." Online posting. 12 January. In *Archives of WPA-L,* January 1999, no. 440 <http://lists.asu.edu/archives/wpa-l.html>.

Simpson, J. 1997. "Re: Writing Centers in English Departments." Online posting. 1 December. In *WCENTER Archives* <http://www.ttu.edu/wcenter/9712/msg00014.html>.

Soja, E. W. 1989. *Postmodern Geographies: The Reassertion of Space in Critical Theory.* New York: Verso.

Tinberg, H. 1999. "Re: Course Loads/Writing Centers." Online posting. 18 January. In *Archives of WPA-L,* January 1999, no. 323 <http://lists.asu.edu/archives/wpa-l.html>.

Tuman, M. C. 1992. *Word Perfect: Literacy in the Computer Age.* Pittsburgh: University of Pittsburgh Press.

Wallace, R. 1998. "Random Memories of the Wired Writing Center: The Modes-to-Nodes Problem." In *Wiring the Writing Center,* edited by E. H. Hobson, 163–70. Logan, UT: Utah State University Press.

9

Political Issues in Secondary School Writing Centers

Pamela B. Childers and James K. Upton

Understanding a need and being able to do something about it may be one of the toughest challenges in secondary education. Whether in public or independent schools, secondary school writing-center directors deal with unique political issues involving teacher contracts, teacher-duty assignments, and faculty perceptions of writing centers. Writing-center directors and their colleagues in public schools have a minimum of twenty-five students per class, and all of them frequently teach at least five classes a day, five times a week. In independent schools, directors and their colleagues have fewer students per class, fewer classes, and/or fewer class meetings per week; however, they put in many more hours after school and on weekends with sports, clubs, evening study halls, dorm duty, dining-hall supervision, and weekend-activities chaperoning. Within these busy contexts, directors understand the need to participate—and to encourage their colleagues to participate—in writing-across-the-curriculum (WAC) activities, such as giving students feedback during the writing process and assisting faculty with creating and evaluating writing activities for their students.

In our visits to other secondary schools and conversations with secondary colleagues throughout the country, we have discovered that our examples aren't unique to our institutions; only the specifics differ. Jim was part of a team involved with the Iowa Writing Project in the 1980s and implemented a controversial and award-winning writing center at Burlington Community High School in Burlington, Iowa, in 1983. Pam worked on WAC with a team promoted by her superintendent, and she created a writing center as part of her graduate work in 1981. This led to a nonfunded, WAC-based center at Red Bank Regional High School in Little Silver, New Jersey. In 1991 she was hired to develop a writing center and WAC program for the McCallie School, a day/boarding school for boys in Chattanooga, Tennessee. Having directed three different writing centers between us, we have learned much about political issues secondary teachers can encounter.

Jim's principal in 1981 was a former language-arts teacher who became interested in establishing a writing center because of Jim's involvement with the Iowa Writing Project. As chair of the language-arts department at Burlington, Jim discussed creating a writing center with his colleagues. After gaining their overwhelming support, he presented the idea to the Curriculum Committee and the Board of Education, who approved $10,000 to explore the possibility of creating a writing center. During the next year he met a number of writing-center directors, sharing experiences and determining what makes writing centers succeed—and sometimes not.

At the end of this year of research and brainstorming, Jim and ten members of the language-arts department developed a mission statement, goals, and procedures for the proposed writing center. At its presentation to the Board of Education in July 1982, the department requested salary and benefits for another language-arts teacher, use of a corner of the upper library, and access to an old Apple IIe and printer, file cabinet, and bookcase. Teachers interested in working in the writing center would be assigned there as part of their regular assignment of six periods out of a seven-period day. They would also volunteer to staff the center before and after school on a rotating basis. However, unexpectedly, the board refused the additional salary line. After lengthy, often heated discussions, the teachers agreed to cover the writing center the first year and volunteer their time before and after school as originally proposed.

Two years earlier, in 1981, Pam and some of her colleagues across the disciplines had started a writing center at Red Bank Regional. Their start was slightly different because the superintendent had invited a cross-disciplinary team to attend a WAC seminar with Robert Parker at Rutgers. Based on this seminar and on Parker's studies published with Nancy Martin in writing and learning across the curriculum (Martin et al. 1976), Pam and history teacher Sue Johnson Hoffmann surveyed the faculty at Red Bank Regional to find out the kinds of writing that students were doing in their classes. They had read a great deal about WAC during this time and were eager to get a program started. At the same time, Pam was working toward her graduate degree in writing at Northeastern University. One of her projects was to design a secondary-school writing center. With proposal in hand, she approached her principal, who found a space beneath the steps in the library to use during lunch periods as a "virtual writing center." The principal donated both a round table and a four-drawer file cabinet to this space. Pam gained the support of teachers across the curriculum to volunteer part of their lunch period once a week to staff the space, then held after-school workshops to train them in responding to student writing. We both had reached a point where administrators and boards of education seemed to support the *idea* of a writing center. And it was here, in translating principle into reality, where the real problems arose.

The Politics of Contracts

For many school districts, a teachers-association contract has become invaluable in protecting all teachers from either mistreatment or favoritism. In the past, mistreatment through extra assignments and duties without compensation was a problem, especially for nontenured faculty. Therefore, many teachers associations handle the negotiation of a contract with health and retirement benefits, collective bargaining, and individual or group grievances. In other schools without teachers associations or unions, contracts are supposedly equitable, but there is no way to grieve or deal with inequities other than going up the chain of command with one's concern. For example, if all English teachers have five classes and a new teacher has been assigned six, then the association will support the new teacher to see that he or she has an equitable load. If all teachers are required to have an extra duty during the day, then they have it. If teachers are required to be at school fifteen minutes before school begins and after it ends, then that is what all teachers must do. In independent schools, such duties as Day Parents and Boarding Parents weekends are required of all teachers in a similar way.

In both of our cases, we had to convince our colleagues that we were not breaking the teachers contract or setting a precedent. This concern was valid because many of us as teachers had been stuck with difficult assignments or forced to perform inappropriate duties because a teacher had set a precedent that the administration was able to use against other teachers. Since both of us were active members of our teachers associations, we did not want to break any rules of the contract. Jim and his colleagues agreed to write letters to both the association and the district bargaining unit indicating that their "center volunteer work complied with the contractual mandate that planning time and pre- and post-student contact time be used for work on school activities." The letter also stated that their actions were "freely taken and were not to be seen as precedent setting or past practices in any way." The association then acknowledged receipt of the letters and sent one to the district bargaining unit stating that the writing-center work met the contract requirements. Each year as part of the bargaining unit meetings, this sidebar on the contract has to be approved.

For Pam, the problem at Red Bank Regional High School was less complicated. In the first year, teachers were merely volunteering part of their lunch periods once a week, and a full-fledged center did not yet exist. However, Pam immediately approached the principal about a possible problem. Fearful of any unnecessary hassles with the association in a year of contract negotiations, the principal agreed to write a letter to the president of the local association and send copies to each volunteer teacher. The letter stated that this volunteer work during part of a lunch period was strictly a pilot program to see if a writing center was needed, and that it would not be setting a precedent for teachers to do anything during their contractually guaranteed full lunch periods. However, the coverage became aligned with the association contract once the writing center was located in a separate physical space. That is, writing-center duty counted as an extra-duty assignment instead of study hall or cafeteria duty, for instance. For those not familiar with standard contractual duties at many secondary schools, faculty have a set number of classroom-teaching assignments and preparations, plus an extra-duty assignment, a planning period, and a lunch period.

But what about independent schools? There is no real bargaining unit per se, although there may be a strong group of outspoken faculty. What seems to be more the case in independent schools is playing one teacher against another. For instance, if a teacher wants something, he or she may be told about all the teachers who are making tremendous sacrifices for the good of the students without whatever he or she wants. If administrators want a teacher to do something, they may tell that teacher about other teachers who have already given up eating to do what they want him or her to do. At McCallie, alumni had created an endowed chair to start a writing center and WAC program. Pam had to take advantage of the "honeymoon" before the money ran out for equipment, space, and employees. She made some correct and incorrect decisions in the process that would affect the writing center and her position politically on campus.

Dealing with Faculty Perceptions

In both of our public school experiences, we were credible people in our institutions; we had been in the trenches, teaching both the best and the brightest as well as the most academically challenged students. Our colleagues saw us working beside them for years. If either of us had arrived as the writing-center director, we would have been seen as a friend of administration and not as a kindred spirit, someone who knows what it is like on the front lines. Language-arts teachers see a new writing-center director as someone who is there because an administrator doesn't think they are doing an adequate job teaching writing. Jim heard a board member say at an Illinois district meeting where teachers proposed a writing center, "We better fire all the English teachers if they're not doing a good enough job teaching writing. We don't need a writing center, we need better English teachers." Is there any wonder why teachers might be suspicious? Pam even had an English department chair tell the entire department that everyone had larger classes because Pam was working in the writing center two periods per day.

A frequent complaint secondary school writing-center workers have heard is that writing-center duty is just "sitting around drinking coffee for an extra period each day." Pam remembers a teacher coming to the door of the writing center and yelling to her, "A student needs help over here!" Pam had been looking at a student's paper when one of the boys on a computer had raised his hand. Later Pam discovered the teacher thought she was dozing when she was actually reading a student paper at her desk.

Why are there so many misconceptions by faculty and administration? Probably the biggest reason is that writing-center directors are usually in very visible spots in an institution, a necessity for student access. Whether in a real or virtual space, directors are subject to the criticism of colleagues who do not know what the directors are doing. Directors must advertise, publicize, think of themselves as public relations people. They have to include as many colleagues as possible in what they do so that directors are not perceived as enemies. This is not an easy task until others see directors working longer hours, making teachers' work easier and supporting what they do. Jim and his volunteers had to prove that they were relieving English teachers of some of their work, yet supporting what they were doing in a positive way. Jim and his volunteers distributed handouts on almost any possible topic that might assist their colleagues without implying, "You are doing this wrong" or "Your assignment doesn't make any sense." The WAC team became proactive and helped with cross-curricular learning activities, creating a file system of writing-to-learn activities to be shared among all staff. They also gave evening seminars for students and parents, but once again these were seen as contract violations, and rumblings continued among faculty, causing one faculty member to resign from the association because it was supporting the writing center and its personnel.

At Red Bank Regional, her public school, Pam spent her professional period in the writing center, skipped lunch many times, and stayed late each day to work with faculty or to prepare materials for classes. She would swap assignments with faculty so that she could go into their classes and give miniworkshops on particular writing problems. She offered poetry workshops by inviting guest artists each year as part of the New Jersey Artists in the Schools and the Geraldine R. Dodge Foundation programs. Teachers across the curriculum could bring their classes to the writing center for such workshops or readings. But some teachers saw all this as having too much fun and suspected that learning couldn't possibly be going on. At McCallie, her independent school, Pam consciously made sure she was seen at her desk before others got there and stayed until after most faculty members had left the academic building. However, many saw her typing on her computer or sitting at her desk reading and responding to student and faculty writing, and they made the assumption that she was not doing anything all day. Before the school was networked, Pam had her assistant work in the writing center first thing in the morning while she stayed at home to use her modem and personal computer. This way she could send student papers and set up exchanges between teachers and students at other schools on her personal e-mail account. She was also actively involved in national conferences, presenting at a maximum of three per year. At the beginning of the next school year, Pam was reprimanded for "coming late," "doing your own personal e-mail at home," and "not being around when you were needed." Needless to say, public relations had to become a more important issue in order to maintain funds to staff the center and update the technology.

Sometimes directors are asked to explain the writing process or research paper in content-specific classes, then serve as a resource, and even grade student papers for correct use of MLA guidelines. Directors have to tolerate almost any request if they want to win converts to their view of writing and learning. What secondary school writing-center directors do consistently is assist students with any phase of the writing process, from prewriting activities through final submissions; to provide writing, writing-to-learn, study skills, and other writing/learning assistance as requested by faculty; and to serve as the center for writing, staff development, and exchange of writing strategies and models. They would probably agree that they spend more time today on staff development activities than they did at the beginning. For instance, when teachers come in to design a research project for their students, they may change the way they teach this activity before the project has been completed. A teacher may decide to let his or her students determine the evaluation criteria; students may summarize each other's research to share in the learning; and the responsibility for checking the research format may fall completely on the writing-center staff. In other words, this teacher may make some major educational paradigm shifts to a more student-centered class because of one writing project.

Another part of secondary school writing-center directors' political position is to sell what they do to students, faculty, administration, and parents. Ideally, if they are effective salespeople, they don't have problems with staffing, funding, and support of the center. Jim's team went about offering not only writing workshops but help with study and learning skills, as mandated by the state. They developed effective general-study skills, content-specific study skills, note-taking and test-taking strategies, and writing process in-class presentations. To attract parent support, they offered study skills and college application essay workshops in the evenings with free pens and pencils provided by local businesses, writing-related books as door prizes, and good refreshments. Pam's staff and students at Red Bank Regional gave in-class workshops, evening readings by guest artists and creative writing majors, college application essay sessions, and a writing-career seminar. At the McCallie writing center, she has offered faculty/student poetry readings with refreshments, workshops for parents, and WAC workshops for faculty in the mentor program. One of her most successful programs has been the private work she does with faculty in preparing grant proposals, working on graduate theses or dissertations, and collaborating on articles or chapters for publication. She has helped students and teachers collaborate on pieces they have had published in professional journals and books.

We both have worked with keyboarding teachers to help students with résumés and business letters; however, Jim has used these students to type writing-center materials, and he has provided copies of student works to the public library, medical offices, and the chamber of commerce. Both of us have also provided writing courses for local businesses that wanted to improve the writing abilities of their middle-management personnel. A large law firm in Chattanooga hired Pam to train its junior partners in writing letters to clients, for instance.

But all of this outside work is not recognized by many secondary-school colleagues and administrators as "helping the school" the way a winning team would. In the last decade enrollments have dropped at many public schools, so writing-center directors have new challenges to keep their centers viable. Jim's center lost funding and his team had to volunteer to work during their planning period. Two members of the team have retired, and fewer teachers have been willing to work during their planning periods. They trained more student tutors so that they could keep the center open during all periods. National Honor

Society students were scheduled whenever possible, and occasionally the staff traded classes to make presentations.

Liability and Staffing Issues

Many schools will not allow students to work in an unsupervised area of the school. Another part of the contract that has to be negotiated between the administration and boards is insurance coverage. That is, since secondary schools serve students who are minors, the school and/or district is responsible for the welfare of its students during the school day. If the school has an "open campus" where students over eighteen are free to leave during lunch periods or when they don't have an assigned class, the parents must sign a release acknowledging this. However, the school is accountable for the whereabouts and safety of its students from the beginning until the end of the school day unless otherwise specified. For instance, if a student gets hit in the eye with a flying paper clip and there is no supervision of the area, then the school is legally at fault. Historically, schools that have had any insurance suits tend to have knee-jerk reactions to anything that even hints at a problem of supervision of students. Jim's center was located in the library area, but the insurance required that a certified staff member be assigned specifically to the writing center, not just to the library in general. To add to the problem, the enthusiastic new fire marshal declared that the center location created a fire hazard and interfered with possible emergency exit from the library. There went that writing center!

Interestingly, Pam's virtual center located first under the steps and then in the office at the top of the steps in the library was considered both safe and within the requirements of the insurance coverage. A certified teacher was assigned to library duty every period, so the student tutors were able to keep the little room open every period by volunteering to cover it while Pam was in classes. When the center grew and was moved to the middle of the English pod, no one considered coverage a problem since the space had windows on the sides that faced other classrooms and the doors remained open whenever Pam left the room.

Another political issue is staffing. We have hinted at this issue when discussing the training of tutors, writing consultants, or peer reader listeners. Both of us have used students in a variety of ways. In our public school situations, we have worked with student volunteers, whether through the National Honor Society or by recommendation from teachers. Most secondary schools cannot pay tutors/consultants. Some schools, public and independent, offer peer tutoring as part of a course. Pam has offered this elective at McCallie for several years, but not many students have time to schedule it. There are usually only a few students willing to take this elective, but the ones who do seem enthusiastic enough about the experience to have published chapters and articles describing their experience working with students across the disciplines. Parent volunteers can create a tricky situation, but we know of schools where retired journalists and writers volunteer to work with the writing-center personnel very effectively. In some districts such as Montclair, New Jersey, two professional writers were hired to train parents to work in writing centers throughout the district. The writers were paid to train writing-center personnel and prepare materials for them to use in working with students. The best and worst writing-center personnel can be professional teachers. Both of us have run into the political situation of knowing that a colleague who wants to work in the writing center will do more harm than good. Sometimes a student being tutored will say to the faculty member, "They don't do that in here. You are supposed to ask me questions to help me discover my own weaknesses or to help me focus on my ideas." When that happens, we may have converted another teacher to our writing-center philosophy. Because Jim started with a strong team of teachers trained in the Iowa Writing Project, he had models for others. His colleagues in the English department spent a great deal of time working with students before and after school, going into classrooms to present ideas on writing, thinking, and learning, and working with other faculty on creating writing activities. Unfortunately, Jim's school no longer has a physical space for a writing center, just a virtual space. That means Jim and the other remaining staff member will have to make some serious decisions as to whether the virtual writing center will be able to do much of anything in the next school year besides visiting classrooms.

At both schools Pam has had to first train both students and faculty across the curriculum, who then helped train those who followed them. She remembers the tenth-grade student who learned how to become a tutor by observing a senior who was not an outstanding writer but a great tutor. The tenth grader presented at the peer-tutoring conference at Bucknell his junior year and got rave reviews from the tutors at Brown University and other colleges in 1985. In fact, when asked by the college tutors how a high-school sophomore could respond to the paper of a senior, he commented that age does not determine if a piece of writing clearly presents information. He knew how to ask about the purpose and audience, and to ask for clarification of information and other such questions because he had been trained well.

For the last seven years at McCallie Pam has relied on a part-time assistant who also teaches composition at the local university and at the secondary school as an adjunct. She had to prove the need before she could get this hourly position funded and continues to fight to get a full-time assistant with benefits. With an assistant covering the physical writing center, she is able to go into classes to teach.

Understanding the Role of Writing Centers

When secondary school writing-center directors look at other forms of writing to improve learning, they are asking teachers to make paradigm shifts in the way they teach and the way students learn. Presentations and workshops by teachers demonstrate what they have done with their classes based on writing-center interaction. Having teachers actually participate in writing workshops where they are practicing what directors hope they will try in their own classes is the most effective way to sell a writing-center program. For instance, one of Pam's science colleagues wanted to design a research activity for a physical science class. By working collaboratively with her, they designed not only the directions for an effective writing activity but also the tool for grading the research activity. Once he tried this lesson and found it effective, three other science teachers came to the writing center to work on writing activities for their classes. Every year teachers are using and revising the activity that that science teacher designed six years ago.

Another political issue is how secondary school writing centers "help" students. Parents think that if their children come to the writing center, they should get better grades on their papers. Both of us make it quite clear up front that we are not responsible for student grades. We are there to help students become better writers, thinkers, and learners; however, help does not guarantee a higher grade on a paper. Also, students quickly learn that we do not "edit" their papers for grammatical errors. When a student handed Pam a paper and asked her to check it for errors, she responded, "You can't afford me as an editor." When the student looked stunned, Pam continued, "But I will be glad to sit down and talk with you about your paper."

Conclusion

How do secondary school writing-center directors function and position themselves within the politics of their institutions? They must constantly keep up on experimenting with innovations, improving and using their faculty and staff more effectively, and trying to be sensitive to the priorities of the school administration, board, and teachers association. These may change as new pedagogies come and go, and as administrators and board members come and go. For example, Jim's physical space does or does not exist, depending on the current administrator and the budget; however, he and his colleagues continue to study and apply new learning ideas. Currently they have been focusing on brain-based learning, researching and developing workshops and materials for faculty and students.

Finally, secondary school writing-center directors cannot deny the effects of social interactions. Whether it is in the school cafeteria, after school with a group at the local watering hole, or at formal gatherings, faculty and administrators learn more about who the directors are, what they do, and how they make teachers look good.

Directors frequently joke about their jobs, saying anyone who wants to work more and get less recognition for all their time and effort should direct a writing center. In many cases this is not far from the truth, although they continue to fight the misconception mentioned at the beginning of this chapter. What has happened and will continue to happen is that directors must keep revising their roles both within and outside the institution of learning to adapt to changes both favorable and unfavorable. But more than that, they must continue to keep themselves informed of what is happening in their profession, in the teaching of writing and directing writing centers, and be prepared for whatever is thrown their way.

Work Cited

Martin, N., P. D'Arcy, B. Newton, and R. Parker. 1976. *Writing and Learning Across the Curriculum* 11–16. London: Ward Lock.

10

An Audit of the National Writing Centers Association's Growth

Eric Hobson and Kelly Lowe

Founded in 1982, the National Writing Centers Association (NWCA) is preparing to head into its third decade of existence in great shape, both financially and politically. According to NWCA's former executive secretary, Joyce Kinkead (1996), the NWCA provides for the writing-center community many important services: increased visibility, networks for information sharing and personal or professional development, and legitimacy in other professional and academic communities. Few writing-center personnel would debate Kinkead's assessment of the benefits to the writing-center community that have come about as a result of NWCA's existence. There is debate, however, about the form that these benefits have taken, and the extent to which they have been enacted over the past two decades. Although a review of the writing-center literature during this twenty-year span reveals pleas and exhortations for NWCA to take on decidedly activist mantles as well as counterclaims of having done just that, a review of minutes from the organization's board meetings and our discussions with past and current NWCA officers and board members demonstrates no consistent pattern of organizational activity in response to such calls.

Until recently, NWCA enjoyed the luxury of appearing to represent a community with fairly homogenous concerns and interests, one in which it was possible to know most members of the NWCA board, just as it seemed possible to know most of the organization's membership. This overriding sense of intimacy encouraged a somewhat informal, decidedly relaxed organizational structure and operating procedures that rested on the assumption that board policy reflected the desires of the membership. Yet, as the NWCA's two-decade anniversary nears, it is worth examining how close the correspondence is between the NWCA's mission and priorities, as defined by the organization's constitution, its officers and board members, and the perceptions and needs of writing-center personnel who are and are not NWCA members. Has this closeness ever been a part of NWCA membership, or is it something just imagined by some of the founders and long-time members?

NWCA is an excellent example of an organization whose success has exceeded its founders' initial projections. Its financial strength, increasing venues for writing-center-based publication, a standing bi-annual conference, expansion of its regional affiliate network to include Europe, and the establishment of the NWCA Press attest to robust organizational growth. But growth, while exciting and rewarding, also strains the community's fabric. In any organization undergoing change, stress occurs between the ways things have been and predictions about the way things should be. There often exists an undercurrent of opinion that the organization created to meet the needs of a specific community has lost its sense of mission or its responsibility to its membership.

The question, on the surface, seems simple: what's so wrong with organizational evolution? NWCA, a large, strong organization, offers the writing-center community greater lobbying power, more money, a press, conferences, publishing opportunities, even research grants. Of course, with this growth come drawbacks: a large membership escalates the potential for a less personal organization, a wide range of member concerns and needs, more competition for money and publications, greater emphasis on specialization, and an increase in theoretical work at, perhaps, the expense of the practical. Development can also alienate the founders as they are moved or pushed aside to make way for the new bureaucrats.

To assess the costs and benefits associated with NWCA's evolution, we examined the NWCA's changing demographics and their effects on its purpose for existing as defined by the first section of the NWCA constitution: support writing-center professionals, advocate for their needs, and extend the body of knowledge about writing-center-based instruction. For the assessment to reflect the varied perspectives of the organization's multiple stakeholders, we surveyed via e-mail three NWCA constituency groups—NWCA presidents, NWCA members, and writing-center personnel who are not NWCA members—using the following questions, which were designed to encourage extended responses:

- How do you define NWCA's mission?
- What has been NWCA's most important activity to date?
- What does NWCA do least effectively?

- How has the writing-center community's growth affected NWCA?
- What role, if any, did NWCA play in this growth/change?
- What benefits result from NWCA membership?
- Has NWCA growth affected affiliate strength?
- Has NWCA's existence changed the flavor of the writing-center community?
- Why should people join and maintain NWCA membership?
- Have we lost anything in the community's push for professionalism?
- What project(s) would you like to see NWCA begin?

Survey responses present an overall positive assessment of NWCA and the writing-center community's growth and development. Responses also reveal more critical assessment in five areas: concern about an insider/outsider divide, questions about the organization's mission and growth, a call for leadership in shaping writing-center scholarship, the need for advocacy, and questions about the assessment role of NWCA.

Insider/Outsider Polarity

The kind of informal structure of NWCA's early years is referred to by Carter McNamara in his essay "Founder's Syndrome: How Founders and Their Organizations Recover" as a "founding structure" that is "vital to the organization's initial start-up and growth" (1998, 38). More often than not, continues McNamara, a typical organization's founders "are dynamic, driven, and decisive. They carry a clear vision of what their [association] can be and are passionate about meeting their [constituents'] needs" (38). Without structural and procedural modifications, these traits, often assets at start-up, can become liabilities as the association develops. McNamara lists several traits that can impede organizational growth:

- skepticism about planning, policies, and procedures
- reactive, crisis-driven decision making
- constant generation of new ideas
- dependence on those who are loyal and/or accessible
- efforts to remove board members who disagree with them.

Many member and nonmember comments in the surveys reflect these particular growing pains. Comments range from displeasure with the "unfriendliness" or "cliquishness" of the board and longtime members, creating the idea that "NWCA represents more accurately its leaders than its broad membership," to the more serious charge that NWCA has "an unclear mission."

It is particularly interesting to note that presidents are more interested in metaissues, such as national status and writing-center assessment, probably as a reflection of their investment in NWCA. Yet presidents are not immune to a sense of diminished contact with the organization and its leaders. Several mention that since leaving the board they too feel "out of the loop," and that NWCA does a poor job of "communicating to members who don't attend national or regional meetings."

A less frequent but more important criticism concerns the perception of "insider" insularity and higher-ed chauvinism. Comments suggest that NWCA serves postsecondary writing-center interests exclusively. While the writing-center community prides itself on its openness and inclusive nature, the *only* survey response from a colleague working in an educational setting other than college or university puts the issue thus: "[NWCA] has become almost an exclusive higher ed organization (maybe it always has been)." This respondent points out that even our method of surveying for this study gives privilege to postsecondary constituencies. Internet access is not always granted to educators working in elementary and secondary schools, and they have little free time to read e-mail, surf the web, or fill out surveys.

Embedded in criticisms that NWCA can appear to foster dichotomies in the writing-center community are comments that attest to respondents' awareness of the many explanations for such perceptions. One response in particular synthesizes such statements:

> My experience with other professional organizations (e.g., WPA and the WAC group) suggests that the most difficult thing to do well is to open an organization to new people—so that new people really feel part of the community, especially during meetings. Open mixing time is a good thing, but mostly for people who are already well-known within the organization. . . . Those who've worked in the [writing center] field for a long time undoubtedly know each other well. . . . But organizations get less comfortable as they get bigger.

There are echoes of nostalgia among many responses for a time when NWCA was a small organization, a sentiment similar to the phenomenon Kinkead (1996) alludes to when she notes that as NWCA grows and becomes a more formal, structured entity, "no doubt old-timers of NWCA will begin to talk sentimentally about the 'early days' of the organization when 'everyone knew everyone else'" (139). The trouble with Kinkead's history is that its predictions are based on rather nostalgic notions of what NWCA's past was like and what its future would be. In her article, Kinkead shows that within its first year, NWCA had 350 members. Since then, the membership has held steady at around 350–450. With these numbers, it is unlikely that at any time "everyone knew everyone else," and it is as unlikely for that to happen in the future. What is more likely is that a core group of founding members knew each other and assumed they knew the bulk of the membership (or projected their founders' closeness on everyone on the roster). Kinkead's comments come from the perspective of a founder, and we're willing to bet that she too has fallen into the "founder's syndrome" that we cite before.

Confusion of Mission

As the survey responses clearly show, NWCA's mission is amorphous, even among presidents where we expected familiarity with the issue. Depending upon who is asked, NWCA's mission is to "encourage and foster the development of writing centers," "support in a variety of ways the continuing development of writing centers in all of their settings," "increase the professionalism of writing center practitioners," "support the scholarship of writing centers in theory and practice," and "provide a national forum for writing center discussion." Of course, these are things that any national advocacy organization should do, and many (and we are among them) would argue that NWCA does the things listed above, although not always in highly visible ways. Kinkead's personal history of NWCA's organizational and cultural history (1996) includes a synthesis of all of the above-mentioned NWCA "missions": advocacy, authority, labor union, theory and praxis championing, and social forum (137–39). However, NWCA stakeholders have always found it difficult to articulate an organizational mission because no such statement exists. As Kinkead rightly observes, "Nowhere in the bylaws of NWCA will these reasons for its existence be made explicit, but they are there, unwritten, evidenced by the actions of the organization" (139).

In articulating their sense of NWCA's mission, the three respondent groups differ in focus. Past presidents define political and advocacy roles for NWCA. The other two respondent groups focus more on NWCA's mission as community building and resource sharing. This difference in mission between these constituency groups reveals differences in how they envision NWCA: past presidents think of the organization in global, managerial terms, as a medium for achieving metagoals; other members of the writing-center community look to the organization as an information clearinghouse and a professional identity anchor point.

Scholarship

When the responses to questions about the rewards and benefits of membership are analyzed, NWCA's encouragement of writing-center scholarly activity emerges as the organization's most valuable contribution to the daily lives of the writing-center personnel who responded. Support for critical reflection and investigation of issues surrounding writing-center instruction and administration—issues about both theory and praxis—has been ongoing and multifaceted. NWCA's support for scholarship spans the organization's history: at its inception in 1982, NWCA allied itself with the two established writing-center publications, the *Writing Lab Newsletter* and *The Writing Center Journal.* The increased professional demands on writing-center directors (especially those who are tenure-track) have created a need for more publication outlets. NWCA has striven to provide such outlets for the dissemination of writing-center-based research through its creation of the standing, biannual NWCA conference and the founding of the NWCA Press. To encourage research leading to publication in these outlets, NWCA offers grant support for graduate research on writing-center issues and maintains a budget line to fund a competitive writing-center research grant.

It would be cynical to say that the only need for publication is to allow people to get tenure, and that brand of justification for more writing-center scholarship was not apparent in respondents' comments. The quality of publication is also important, and respondents acknowledge NWCA's activities designed to taking the lead on this issue as well, with one individual specifically noting, "I think the quality of writing center scholarship has also improved greatly over the past few years."

Survey responses, however, once again highlight a difference of perspective that exists between how presidents think about NWCA's role in encouraging scholarly activity and how other stakeholders think about the issue. In her presentation at the NWCA conference in Park City, Utah, Christina Murphy galvanized the audience when she assessed the current state of writing-center research as "bankrupt." While no respondent goes as far as Murphy did, there is a consensus that NWCA plays an important role in helping to set the writing-center community's research agenda. What that agenda should look like differs, however, depending on whom you ask. NWCA rank and file and nonmembers deal with this issue more generically than do presidents. Whereas the first two groups appreciate NWCA's support for the journals and the NWCA Press, see real value in the annual dispensing of writing-center scholarship awards, and look forward to being able to apply for funds to support their research, presidents are much more specific in what that research should look like. The following response is particularly representative:

> I would like us to sponsor collaborative research projects among directors on different academic levels. These projects should receive financial support and culminate in publication by NWCA Press. That way we could all learn from the research and scholarship of our colleagues.

The national organization has a real opportunity to provide leadership in this area. One president focuses close attention on the role that NWCA can and should play (especially through its two journals) in pressing for more rigorous scholarship—empirical studies, theoretical positioning, and so on—while also maintaining its longstanding habit of helpful, practice-based scholarship. "[It's] time," writes the individual, "to get away from cookies in the writing center articles of *WLN* [the *Writing Lab Newsletter*] and move to the Murphy, Hobson, Carino 'hard' research articles."

Advocacy

In contrast to the support for scholarship, NWCA's efforts at formal advocacy have been sporadic. While NWCA endorsed Jeanne Simpson's 1985 *The Writing Center Journal* article, "What Lies Ahead for Writing Centers: Position Statement on Professional Concerns," and the writing-center community cheered Valerie Balester's contribution to the 1992 *College Composition and Communication* symposium on professional standards, "Revising the 'Statement': On the Work of Writing Centers," the NWCA has focused more of its energies on less formal, more immediate forms of advocacy. Instead of filling the National Council of the Teachers of English (NCTE) board meetings with resolution statements, NWCA officers and members have willingly engaged in information and resource sharing, often to help a colleague meet eleventh-hour ultimatums for job justifications, provide statistics about "usual" writing-center use, or prevent attempts to slash center operating budgets.

Increasingly, professional organizations are being called upon to adopt advocacy positions. Witness, for example, the fight within the Modern Language Association (MLA) over its desire not to get involved in the dire hiring situation within English studies, or, perhaps on a more national level, the NCTE's work on the national standards project. More recently, the Council of Writing Program Administrators has been involved in the process of releasing a statement on outcomes for first-year writing classes. It has long had a statement of professional standards that is given to every new member and periodically distributed to members at the Conference on College Composition and Communication (CCCC). It is also available on its website and has appeared from time to time in the organization's journal, *WPA: Writing Program Administration*. These organizations, with their similar missions, might stand as good examples as NWCA grows. One of the president's surveys goes right to the heart of this matter, responding, "NWCA should . . . be a national voice for writing center professionals, taking stands on critical issues and giving writing centers the kind of support which will help them function in their own institutions." How the NWCA does this can take a variety of shapes, and it will be up to the board and the membership over the next few years to shape and define what sort of advocacy role that NWCA takes.

Writing-Center Assessment

Perhaps no issue right now is more hotly debated, at least within the writing-center community, than assessment. Many surveys mention the desire for the NWCA to become an assessment body, akin, we assume, to the Council of Writing Program Administrators consultant-evaluator service. The question, of course, is whether the NWCA wants to get into this kind of business. Opinions are mixed. While the members are largely in favor of it, the presidents, with a few exceptions, are very much against it. Our survey data, minutes from NWCA board meetings, and private conversations with board members, constituent members, and past presidents are inconclusive about why accreditation is such a difficult issue for NWCA to take on. Time, money, initial certification, and mission all get brought up again and again in an unending Catherine wheel of doubt and blame. This is an area that the NWCA will be watching closely in the next few years.

Study Limitations

An obvious weakness of this survey and its administration is the exclusive use of the Internet. Calls for participation were distributed via the writing-center electronic-discussion group WCenter (wcenter@ lyris.ttu.edu) and the NWCA Executive Board listserv NWCA-L (nwca-l@postoffice.cso.uiuc.edu). The survey instruments (one for NWCA members and nonmembers and one for NWCA presidents) were located on a web page housed at Mount Union College.

Online surveying was chosen as the data collection route for the following reasons:

- WCenter subscribes about 550 NWCA members and nonmembers, thus providing access to a potential participant pool otherwise not readily accessible.
- Java scripts allow for immediate coding and sorting of survey data.
- Online surveying does not incur postage costs and response times are shorter.
- We were curious about how willing our colleagues would be to respond to a web-based survey.

While these reasons for using the Internet as a survey medium are justified, they do open the data to questions of self-selection, a concern that is warranted in light of the overall unanimity of responses. Although not surprising, the uniformly positive responses nevertheless were unexpected; given the self-selective nature of the respondent pool, we anticipated that we would elicit more varied responses than we did. No respondent found NWCA to be anachronistic, obsolete, self-absorbed, dangerous, misrepresenting of their needs, and so on. The choice to recruit respondents from WCenter may account for the positive responses. People who desire an activist writing-center community, for example, find the chatty, highly personal nature of most WCenter messages and conversations frustrating and counterproductive. Many of these potential "naysayer" respondents may have removed themselves from the WCenter roster and, thus, did not receive the survey.

Final Audit

The chances are quite good that NWCA is no longer exactly the organization that its founders thought that they were bringing into existence. Their expectations set the agenda, as Kinkead detailed, for the organization's first decade of growth. The second decade of growth has shown that the organization must evolve into a more formal, managed entity if it is to continue to meet the increasingly complex expectations of its stakeholders. Yet, in the midst of that evolution from Kinkead's *kaffeeklatsch* (1996, 138) to McNamara's postfounder's organization, NWCA will be remiss if it fails to remember the important role that NWCA has played in the evolution of the writing-center community as a whole, and vice versa. One president assesses the reciprocity of this situation quite eloquently:

I think [NWCA] exists because of the writing center community. All the NWCA leaders are writing center workers, and they have made the organization a strong one because of a bottom-up approach, a true collaboration between writing center workers and writing center leaders. We need to ensure that as growth continues, new voices are welcomed and veteran voices are maintained. Without this, NWCA runs the risk of becoming monolithic and autocratic.

Of course, the risk of becoming monolithic and autocratic is the very difficulty NWCA is going to have to face up to as it approaches its third decade of service—the NWCA needs to assess its power and attendant responsibility to that power. NWCA has already done the easy things: developed and supported meetings, scholarships, a press. All that's left are the "hard" things: accreditation, lobbying, a mission statement (with goals and assessments), and an expanded, diverse membership that will have, we assume, expanded and diverse expectations, needs, and desires.

Flash cut to the April 1999 NWCA board meeting. Several long-running issues are on the floor: a name change to International Writing Centers Association, accreditation, the static membership, and so forth. The votes on these issues should be one of two things—contentious battles with members entrenched within their positions, or mere formalities, the details of the agreements having been worked out before the meeting. But they are neither. The debates (some of which have been going on for years) go around in a circle, ultimately leading to no decisions. Items are tabled, sent to committee, reworked. But nothing is voted on. Why?

The NWCA has been, for almost twenty years, a collection of nice people doing nice work. As with any organization, success can be as damaging and paralyzing as failure. The unstated assumption of many members—that NWCA is a nonpolitical organization—is becoming increasingly hard to justify. Its trepidation about politicizing itself is understandable but unacceptable. Our worry, as we look at the results of our surveys and attempt to piece together the narrative they represent, is that if the NWCA doesn't politicize itself, it will be politicized by external forces or will implode under the weight of its own atavistic desire to remain forever rooted in the good old days.

Works Cited

Balester, V. 1992. "Revising the 'Statement': On the Work of Writing Centers." *College Composition and Communication* 43 (2): 167–71.

Kinkead, J. 1996. "The National Writing Centers Association as Mooring: A

Personal History of the First Decade." *The Writing Center Journal* 16 (2): 131–43.

McNamara, C. 1998. "Founder's Syndrome: How Founders and Their Organizations Recover." *Nonprofit World* 16 (6): 38–41.

Simpson, J. 1985. "What Lies Ahead for Writing Centers: Position Statement on Professional Concerns." *The Writing Center Journal* 5 (2): 35–39.

11

Lining Up Ducks or Herding Cats?

The Politics of Writing Center Accreditation

Jeanne H. Simpson and Barry M. Maid

A writing center attached to an English department became vulnerable when an unannounced administrative move merged the department with foreign languages, sent the writing-center-friendly English department chair packing, and imposed a single, traditional rhetoric textbook on all sections for first-year writing. A well-established writing center at a small liberal arts college lost its funding. A five-year-old writing center was abruptly merged with a developmental lab led by a director who espoused an error-correction pedagogy. A writing center at a major land-grant university suffered from a revolving-door directorship, held successively by senior graduate assistants and temporary staff who sought faculty status at other institutions as quickly as possible. In all these cases, cries for help appeared on the WCenter listserv. Advice and sympathy flowed immediately: make your case this way; talk to that person; gather these statistics.

Every year, this pattern of battles for survival continues in the writing-center community. Fighting these battles over and over again, individually, even with the virtual assistance of listserv colleagues, reflects a failure to address the inherent vulnerability of writing centers as academic support programs. There has to be a better way to ensure the success—and not merely the survival—of writing centers than to depend on the luck and savvy of individual directors and the unpredictable goodwill of administrations toward the concept of writing centers.

The current situation for writing centers, if one is to judge from these listserv messages and commentary from various directors, is one of relatively low institutional status and limited access to resources and support. Writing centers remain vulnerable to budget crisis and to administrative turnover. Too often the director must make a case for the writing center in the circumstances of emergency, when the threats are immediate and drastic. Spending energy and the already limited political capital of the writing center to fight fires instead of gathering support for expansion and progress contributes to the frustration that afflicts many writing-center directors.

The preferred situation would be one in which a writing center has a clearly defined and well-supported role within an institution. The center would not be vulnerable to the vagaries of personnel changes in upper administration or to budgetary skids. The center would enjoy an academic reputation commensurate with that of other programs directly connected to the curriculum and would not have to prove its value unexpectedly or inappropriately.

What obstacles exist between the current situation and the preferred situation, and how might writing-center personnel remove or overcome those obstacles?

The low institutional status of the writing center is the most obvious obstacle. How much writing-center directors actually desire to remove this obstacle and how much they fear doing so are far less obvious. On the one hand, the sudden threat of eliminating programs and positions galvanizes action. On the other hand, writing-center directors perceive themselves as being agents of change in their institutions, so compliance with administrative priorities and initiatives may be at odds with this self-perception. Thus a second, less apparent obstacle to the preferred situation may be resistance to change or to accepting the values of the academic establishment. There is a safety in low institutional status, for it protects revolutionary or subversive ideas with the shield of obscurity (Simpson, Braye, and Boquet 1994).

We argue here for accreditation as a means to ensuring the preferred situation. However, the willingness of the writing-center community to accept this option is not clear. Resistance to the idea of accreditation seems to have several sources. One is political naïveté. Writing-center personnel often are prevented, either by inexperience or by institutional location, from having much political understanding of their institutions. Another source is the commingling of personal aspirations of writing-center directors and the institutional mission of the writing center, so that they seem to be the same thing, though in reality they are not. A third source is fear of enmeshing the writing-center community in a structure that seems rigid and perhaps not suitable to the flexible style of writing centers. And a final source is fear of the demands of an expensive and time-intensive bureaucracy for accomplishing and supervising accreditation processes.

Part of the reason the same battles are fought over and over, with only the institutional names changing, is that most writing-center professionals focus primarily on serving students and fail to address the political realities of their institutions. Until writing-center professionals collectively come to terms with the fact that their individual centers will always be a part of the political landscape, WCenter will continue to receive posts of "cries in the night." We believe that the best way of assuring continued quality academic service to students while solidifying writing centers' positions within their individual institution's political structures is accreditation.

A well-designed accreditation process would provide a framework for defending writing centers that does not presently exist. Accreditation is, by definition, a process that is applied to individual programs but which represents a global vision of what such programs can and should be. At present, a body of scholarship (see Murphy, Law, and Sherwood 1996) offers elements of such a vision, but the works defining writing-center mission and theory are aimed at other writing-center personnel. Inviting administrators to read these works amounts to asking them to become experts so they will agree with writing-center goals. The time constraints alone mitigate against this as an effective strategy—no administrator wants to read a long scholarly article in an unfamiliar field, even one as readable as Stephen North's "The Idea of a Writing Center" (1984), in order to be proved wrongheaded.

The problem of offering a reasonable defense of a writing center is compounded by two additional factors. First, writing centers often do not generate student credit hours or any other direct, measurable form of productivity, while they do consume institutional resources, including salaries, commodities, and space. They neither conform to the standard academic model of departments nor have students who major in "writing center." Furthermore, the research and service activities of a writing-center director do not always resemble those of other faculty. Meanwhile, administrators find oddball structures to be complicating factors as policies and procedures don't quite fit or reporting lines are unusual. If *output,* to use a term writing-center directors generally loathe but which is in the minds of administrators, is not clearly commensurate with resources invested, an oddball unit is going to be in danger, whether immediately apparent or not (Simpson 1995).

Second, writing-center work seems to attract people who are by nature student-centered and idealistic (Healy 1995). While these admirable qualities result in inventive instructional methods and ideas, at the same time they contribute to political naïveté about academic institutions. Writing-center personnel tend to believe the goodness of writing centers is self-evident because writing centers conform to their own value systems. To find that others do not share that perception produces a shock. The specific status of many directors, who may be graduate students, adjunct faculty, or temporary instructors with low or no rank, exacerbates the problem as these persons often lack a full understanding of the institution's political structures. Their status can prevent them from significant participation in those structures. They are unaware that anyone might have a vested interest in their failure and do not understand why such an interest might exist.

Even in the best of situations and with the best of intentions, the political nature of staffing writing centers often causes political difficulties within an institution. Recently, while visiting a large university with a well-regarded rhetoric and composition program, Barry Maid met with the graduate student directing the center. One of the topics of concern the director expressed to Maid was the increasing battle for funding. Later, discussing the matter with the director of composition (a tenured faculty member), Maid suggested that the whole writing program would be better served if the writing-center director were also a tenured faculty member. The composition director responded by explaining that the administrative work was wonderful training for graduate students and helped them to find good jobs after graduation. Maid acknowledged the sincerity and accuracy of this statement, but then he asked, "And how much clout does your graduate student writing-center director have with your provost when he goes to ask for money?" The composition director could only reply that the graduate student never got in to see the provost.

Retelling Maid's anecdote is not an argument that all writing-center directors need to be tenured faculty. However, it does emphasize the point that until other academic capital is brought into play, such as accreditation, tenured directors are one of the few viable political options. Indeed, political reasons such as access and credibility with upper administration drive a common response to political pressures, the notion that writing-center directors should be tenure-line faculty (Simpson 1985; Cobb 1989; Elliott 1990). This response fails to recognize that every tenure-line position has to be negotiated at any institution. Blending the battle for a tenure-line position with the battle to protect a writing center often complicates the problem rather than solving it. It leaves the battle to be fought by one individual, with only moral support available from the writing-center community. No amount of referenced scholarship or e-mail and letter campaigns from other directors will result in a tenure-line position for anybody; that negotiation is, ultimately, one-to-one. Worse, the individual is generally not in the power position in this negotiation. The administration wields the power; the individual wanting access to tenure is, until tenure is granted, a supplicant. Moreover, asking for a tenure-line position raises the stakes for the administration, as they are now being pushed not only to support a program without much discernible output, but also to commit to a tenure-line position, with its concomitant high, long-term costs. The negative response is entirely predictable and yet consistently unanticipated.

A second problem with the idea that writing-center directors should be tenure-line faculty is that it flies in the face of a deeply held, widely shared principle of writing-center work: context is everything (Crump 1992). In some instances, the directorship may need to be a staff position—a writing center located in a student-services division would be an obvious instance. There is no one-size-fits-all format for either a writing center or its directorship.

This analysis of tenure-line issues reveals another source of the resistance to accreditation. Writing-center directors often confuse their own professional aspirations with the best interests of the writing center itself as an institutional component. Desiring tenure, especially if one's job status is temporary or not clearly housed within a discipline or department, is reasonable and understandable. Further, tenure has long been defined as the most significant status marker in the academy. Unfortunately, tenure is seldom granted outside the structure of an established academic department. For most writing-center personnel, the department that would grant tenure is the English department.

While English departments frequently are hotbeds of political subversion in terms of theory and criticism, their own internal, academic politics tend to remain steadfastly conservative. The place a writing center might fill within such a structure may not fit particularly well with the aspiration of an individual seeking tenure. Writing-center faculty frequently complain of being torn between the traditional research requirements for tenure and the realities of their day-to-day duties. Worse, they find themselves unable to negotiate successfully for support of the writing center for fear of endangering their chances for tenure. The existence of writing-center scholarship has no weight with their literarily inclined colleagues.

An accreditation process would lend credibility to writing-center scholarship. The existence of a professional organization with authority to grant accreditation means that there also exist writing-center scholars and a body of theory and research that has achieved wide acceptance, making it far less easy for evaluators to dismiss the work of writing-center personnel up for retention or tenure. On the other hand, placing one's scholarly efforts in the writing-center arena, especially with an accreditation system in place, may mean the possibility that their English department colleagues will never fully accept their membership in the department. Accreditation of writing centers by writing-center personnel may mean accepting a permanent condition of "other-ness" within their own academic units but without the element of victimhood or marginalization. The barriers between writing centers and English (and other) departments could become less, not more, per-meable if the step of accreditation is taken. The concerns of individuals with regard to this issue complicate the question of accreditation.

While it is clear that some individual efforts to save and strengthen writing centers have succeeded, the strategies that led to these successes are transmitted to others only irregularly, by means of conference papers or WCenter discussions, by letters or telephone calls. The writing-center community's urge to be helpful, to reach out to others who experience the same struggles, is undeniably strong. Its perception of itself as a close-knit community is an asset that has resulted in a national organization and a national conference. The calls for help that appear on WCenter also reflect a belief in the power of collective effort.

If individual efforts are not consistently effective and if a belief in collective power exists, how might the collective power be harnessed to address the vulnerability of writing centers? Certainly, the national and regional writing-center groups represent collective strength. So far, that strength has been used to affirm the concepts and methodolo-gies of writing centers, to share "war stories" and discoveries, and to develop scholarship. These efforts have served to end the sense of iso-lation that early writing-center directors often experienced. From them has emerged the indispensable element of a successful collective effort: a shared, articulated philosophy of purpose and pedagogy for writing centers.

That element has been directed inwardly, used to bond writing-center personnel to each other and to guide initiates or beginners. These are important functions, precisely because so often writing-center personnel are new to the concepts and activities of writing centers. Directorships of academic support services are obvious slots for temporary appointments, for rotating appointments, or for rela-tively junior faculty, creating a constant supply of novices. While there are certainly examples of directors who have moved up through the academic ranks while retaining the directorship for many years, the more common pattern is a three- to five-year directorship, after which the person moves on or out. The whole writing-center community is characterized by a mix of "newbies" and what might be called grizzled veterans combined with those who are no longer novices but who are also not likely to stay for more than a few years. Those who move on to more senior administrative positions—department chair, dean, assis-tant provost—consistently report epiphanies as they gain greater political insight and administrative experience. "If only I had known, when I directed the writing center" is a common refrain.

There is no reason to anticipate any significant change in this mix, as the evidence of questions and issues raised in two decades' worth of writing-center scholarship makes clear. As veterans become so grizzled that they have to retire, others will take their places. Recurring populations of newbies will always be with us. And so will the moderately experienced. The situation will remain stable, even while the persons occupying those niches change as the generations proceed. And if this mix persists, then the problem is one of developing a strategy for using collective power that transcends the constant presence of novices.

The bonding work of the writing-center community has, unfortunately, also resulted in a shared and frequently articulated hostility toward administration. The community perceives administration as the enemy and frames the lack of administrators' knowledge about writing centers and writing-center pedagogy as at least contemptible and often as malevolent. That an economics or biology professor turned provost or dean would have no reason to know anything about writing centers seems not to be a consideration. When more traditional (and familiar) models of writing pedagogy are favored by administrators, the writing-center community may express outrage at the perceived obstructionism. The writing-center community's attempts to provide more accurate information or to offer research-based alternatives often come either too late or are presented defensively. Perceiving a "marginalization" of writing centers, the community attaches blame to administration for failure to be supportive or interested or understanding.

The rhetoric of this hostile attitude has not served the writing-center community effectively. Curiously, writing centers do not consistently extend how they teach writing to teaching administration about themselves; they neither accept the possibility of alternative, valid perceptions nor understand the effects of misinformation. The attitude of authoritative knowledge—I am the teacher and I know best—seems to prevail in this instance. The pedagogical stance of most writing-center professionals does not favor authoritative, dogmatic, or judgmental approaches. And yet, in communications with administration, these approaches seem to be the default. Why? Because the human tendency is to demonize whoever holds power. The balance of power is tilted so heavily toward administration, there seems to be no other option but resistance, even though resistance then leads to the outcome most feared.

Casting the administration into the role of oppressor or malignant authority figure misses the reality: institutions have to be administered and the people assigned to the administrative tasks must meet their obligations just as surely as the writing-center director must. Understanding the situation from the administrative perspective clarifies the equations of authority, budget responsibilities, accountability to external constituencies, and competing demands on limited resources. Administrators may have tenure in an academic department, but they do not ever have tenure in their administrative positions. They hold those positions at the "pleasure" of the next higher authority. They do not have the option of ignoring directives and priorities that come from above, and they must present the results of their decisions and actions in terms that these authorities understand and use.

Can the balance of power be shifted or at least improved to the advantage of the writing center? Can the collective power be brought to bear to accomplish that shift? And if so, how?

If a writing center's existence or structure is threatened, the following criteria might provide for a workable, effective response:

- credibility with faculty and administration
- minimal reliance on informal support systems
- flexibility to accommodate varying contexts
- use of extant expertise
- use of extant collective energies
- minimal reliance on individual effort or rhetorical style
- consonance with the shared, articulated philosophy and methodology of writing centers.

A system for accreditation of writing centers could meet all these criteria.

Accreditation, in spite of the difficulties accrediting bodies are currently experiencing, remains the currency of the academic realm. Schools of business seek AACSB accreditation, and teacher-certification programs seek NCATE accreditation. Often, institutions assign released time to individuals to prepare for accreditation site visits, and the self-study component of accreditation efforts spurs curriculum review and equipment purchases. Provosts and deans pay for the travel expenses of site visitation teams. And new hires may be required to document credentials from accredited programs. All of these actions reflect the value placed on accreditation.

Why does all this occur? Because accreditation implies the existence of standards, of regular external and internal review—in short, quality control. Accreditation is perceived as equivalent to admission to the bar before practicing law or board certification for physicians. Essentially, it answers local political attacks by providing a context that is more than local.

Accreditation relies on collective expertise. An accredited program addresses shared principles, goals, and considerations. It provides a structure for peers who are expert in a field to consult, but does so in a focused manner that requires disinterested professionalism. While cronyism undoubtedly occurs within accreditation systems, it is not openly accepted or expected. Accreditation meets the interests of the experts in a discipline by validating the discipline's core values while at the same time meeting the interests of an institution by supplying a mechanism for assessment and quality control.

A fundamental administrative concern is to be able to verify that resources have been spent wisely and appropriately. A fundamental concern for disciplinary practitioners—in this instance, writing-center personnel—is respect for the body of knowledge and expertise they share with peers. Accreditation procedures can address both these concerns. The mission of writing centers is often defined, in Stephen North's words, as making "sure that writers, and not necessarily their texts, are what get changed by instruction . . . to produce better writers, not better writing" (1984, 438). Writing-center practitioners know that "better writers" means writers who command a variety of writing strategies, who have a realistic model of the writing process, who understand and apply the concepts of purpose and audience. Explaining that definition to administrators or faculty from unrelated disciplines constantly challenges writing-center and writing-across-the-curriculum (WAC) directors. An accreditation process means that all parties accept the validity of the expertise. The struggle to protect a writing center's existence and activities automatically moves to a different level when the expertise it represents is already acknowledged and does not have to be defended. The conversation moves toward issues of appropriate configurations and resources and away from error-correction versus rhetorical principles. The criterion of using collective expertise thus can be met.

The existence of collective expertise does not, however, imply the existence of collective agreement that accreditation for writing centers is an appropriate action for the profession to take. While the political logic of using accreditation to strengthen writing centers in their institutions may be apparent, the writing-center community has clearly demonstrated reservations about this option. Kevin Davis (1999), for example, has pointed to possible legal implications, fearing a suit if accreditation were denied. The capacity of the National Writing Centers Association (NWCA) to support training for accreditation teams and the logistics of accreditation—or assessment processes—seems limited at this time. Getting institutional support for writing-center personnel to receive training and to take time off for site visits is regarded as a significant problem. After more than two years of exploring the option of accreditation, at its 1999 business meeting in Bloomington, Indiana, the NWCA board voted not to support accreditation but to encourage assessment processes as an alternative.

Certainly this action makes any accreditation process unlikely for the near future. Individuals cannot constitute themselves as accrediting agencies, however much they may believe in the usefulness of the concept. The only entity with the credibility to support accreditation at this time is NWCA. Individual consultations and assessments can certainly assist with struggles such as the threat to its existence that Merrimack College's writing center recently faced, but, as Karl Fornes (1999) asked on the WCenter listserv, "Will anyone at Merrimack care about what they have to say?"

We believe this action by the NWCA board reflects the troubling realities of the writing-center profession. There is consensus on the mission of writing centers but no consensus on how to proceed to a different level of professional development and status. The problems cited—lack of institutional support for writing-center personnel to travel and receive training, lack of NWCA facilities to support accreditation, legal vulnerability—are not theoretically based. They are acknowledgment of logistical problems, problems that other organizations have solved.

Without denying that these would be significant problems, we believe that NWCA also could solve them. After all, many have started writing centers with little more than promises and hope. It is not necessary to use the model of a large, inflexible bureaucracy with a long and rigid list of standards. The scale of the enterprise is already different from the enterprise of accrediting a credential-granting program such as teacher certification.

Our experience with institutional support for accreditation efforts is that deans and provosts consistently commit funds for these purposes, perceiving them as being direct means of strengthening quality. In the July 2, 1999, *The Chronicle of Higher Education* article "A State Transforms Colleges with 'Performance Funding,'" Peter Schmidt describes how South Carolina measures accountability. One method is the accreditation of degree-granting programs; accreditation is now required for all programs covered by recognized accrediting bodies. While we do not endorse this approach, the existence of this law suggests the authority that accreditation is perceived to have. Provosts regard faculty participation in site visits to other campuses as acceptable forms of research and professional service, not least because doing so means the faculty member must be well informed and up to date in the discipline.

The South Carolina model does reflect a version of the academy that many would rather not see. On June 28, 1999, Lisa Ede remarked on the WCenter listserv, "In this time of the university as corporation and students as clients, I fear that setting up an accreditation mechanism would add fuel to fires that I would rather see tamped down, rather than ignited. I think . . . some good points [have been presented] about the ways in which accreditation does not necessarily have to lead to standardization. Still, in an era of accountability and outcomes-based assessment, I fear that the accreditation mechanism could be misused."

We agree that the opportunity for misuse exists, certainly if the process is not carefully constructed and, most important, controlled by writing-center personnel. It needs to have both internal and external credibility. It needs to be flexible while still representing a high standard of quality. However, writing centers also must consider the salient fact of the South Carolina model: it was made into law by the state legislature. There is no use pretending that the academy had much if any influence on how it came into being; and however much some other circumstance might be preferred, the reality is that the academic programs of South Carolina are now legally obligated to accountability and assessment. The portent for other states is all too clear.

We also point to the frequent political struggles for mere survival, rather than for the improvement of quality, that afflict writing centers, even after a half century of history. If writing-center professionals choose not to go down the path of accreditation as a means to address this problem, then they should understand the reasons thoroughly and acknowledge them, including the fears and the politics of their own organizations. They need to acknowledge that they may prefer the status quo because they know its details, however uncomfortable they are. They may have to accept their own denial that the status quo cannot be sustained. They may have to acknowledge that they prefer to accept suffering than to change anything. They may have to acknowledge that they prefer to keep their professional organization relatively uncomplicated, that they prefer their low institutional profiles, and that they prefer to direct their energies into the writing center's day-to-day activities and not into long-term efforts.

We do not reject these realities, but we do insist upon acknowledging them. Our argument is ultimately very simple: if the existence of writing centers is already fraught with risk and unpredictability, why not try accreditation as a means to strengthen them? If external powers, such as legislatures and governing boards, exert directly and specifically their power over academic institutions, then writing centers should recognize that these chosen currencies must be writing-center currencies also. If the currency is accountability, assessment, and accreditation, then writing centers already know that they have few options. Quantitative, measurable quality indicators for writing centers are difficult to achieve. The one means already endorsed by the external powers and subject to writing center control is accreditation.

Works Cited

Cobb, L. 1989. "Addressing Professional Concerns." *Writing Lab Newsletter* 13 (7): 11–12.

Crump, E. 1992. "Voices from the Net: Grappling with Institutional Contexts." *Writing Lab Newsletter* 17 (3): 10–12.

Davis, K. 1999. "Re: As the Writing Center Turns, or Survival!" Online posting. 17 June. In *WCENTER Archives* <http://www.ttu.edu/wcenter/9906/msg00105.html>.

Ede, L. 1999. "Re: As the Writing Center Turns, or Survival!" Online posting. 30 June. Forwarded to WCENTER from WCENTR-L, 28 June 1999 <WCENTR-L@lists.missouri.edu>.

Elliott, M. A. 1990. "Writing Center Directors: Why Faculty Status Fits." *Writing Lab Newsletter* 14 (7): 1–4.

Fornes, K. 1999. "Re: As the Writing Center Turns, or Survival!" Online posting. 17 June. In *WCENTER Archives* <http://www.ttu.edu/wcenter/9906.msg00102.html>.

Healy, D. 1995. "Writing Center Directors: An Emerging Portrait of the Profession." *WPA: Writing Program Administration* 18 (3): 26–43.

Murphy, C., J. Law, and S. Sherwood. 1996. *Writing Centers: An Annotated Bibliography*. Westport, CT: Greenwood Press.

North, S. 1984. "The Idea of a Writing Center." *College English* 46 (5): 433–46.

Schmidt, P. 1999. "A State Transforms Colleges with 'Performance Funding.'" *The Chronicle of Higher Education*, 2 July.

Simpson, J. 1995. "Perceptions, Realities, and Possibilities: Central Administration and Writing Centers." In *Writing Center Perspectives*, edited by B. L. Stay, C. Murphy, and E. H. Hobson, 48–52. Emmitsburg, MD: NWCA Press.

———. 1985. "What Lies Ahead for Writing Centers: Position Statement on Professional Concerns." *The Writing Center Journal* 5 (2): 35–39.

Simpson, J., S. Braye, and E. Boquet. 1994. "War, Peace, and Writing Center Administration." *Composition Studies/Freshman English News* 22 (1): 65–95.

12

The Disappearing Writing Center Within the Disappearing Academy

The Challenges and Consequences of Outsourcing in the Twenty-First Century

Christina Murphy and Joe Law

In "On the Road to Recovery and Renewal: Reinventing Academe," William G. Tierney (1998) discusses the challenges that numerous institutions in American society have faced in this century and raises the question: "Whither academe?" (93). Tierney is not alone in his concerns; in fact, theorists tell us that higher education is undergoing a vast epistemological change that will redefine the role of education in America (Benjamin and Carroll 1998; Chaffee 1998; O'Brien 1998; Slaughter and Leslie 1997). This "tectonic shift," as George Dennis O'Brien describes it in *All the Essential Half-Truths About Higher Education* (1998, xii), results from the decline of the postmodern research university as many of its functions, roles, and domains are assumed by other institutional aspects of the culture. In the late twentieth century and early twenty-first, the elimination of the barriers between academics and the postindustrial business and technology complex has created a university with allegiances to academics, to business and technology, and to the societal possibilities generated by these multiple coalitions and affiliations (Chaffee; O'Brien; Slaughter and Leslie). As Sheila Slaughter and Larry Leslie note, "Increasingly, universities compete in complex environments" (227), and, as a consequence, revolutionary transformations of the social goals for education are redefining the practices and purposes of higher education in America.

We believe that the same transformation of higher education's environment is occurring in the writing center. In fact, we contend that the writing center is a microcosm of the changes and redefinitions that the academy itself is now undergoing as the primary purpose of higher education shifts in the postmodern age from an earlier "moralizing mission" of edification and uplift (O'Brien 1998, xiv) to the pursuit of "a different kind of social relevance" based upon "new social partnerships" with the external agencies and audiences the academy serves (Braskamp and Wergin 1998, 62–63).

Clearly, the most dramatic and immediate transformation the writing center faces in the next decade is outsourcing, which will be the strongest force in determining the "different kind of social relevance" and "new social partnerships" the writing center will experience in the twenty-first century. Certainly, the writing center and higher education have experienced a small measure of outsourcing through the influence of technology, which has reduced the need for an academic site or location for classrooms, writing centers, and even the face-to-face contact of students with teachers, tutors, or fellow classmates. The wide-scale introduction of technology into education and the extensive use of the Internet have diminished the need for an actual location for academic instruction and have made instruction "mobile" or "portable" to multiple locations and audiences. In *The Digital Economy: Promise and Peril in the Age of Networked Intelligence*, Donald Tapscott (1996) describes this change as "virtualization" and identifies it as a major theme central to the new "digital economy" of the Information Age (43–72). Virtualization frees writing centers and writing programs from the limitations of being housed in physical spaces on campuses. Online writing labs (OWLs) represent one application of virtualization to writing instruction, and they presage future trends in the movement away from the concept of the writing center as an academic location toward a "writing center" of global access.

The next step in the outsourcing of education will occur as the educational functions traditionally assigned to the academy are taken over by external agencies. For writing centers, outsourcing will have a twofold impact. First, much of the work of the academy will be privatized as it is outsourced to competing businesses. For Tapscott (1996), this is an example of "disintermediation," which involves the elimination of intermediaries in economic activity—in essence, the classic elimination of the middle man (56–58). Disintermediation is one of the key likelihoods facing writing centers. A scenario in which writing programs within the academy are disintermediated by the business and professional communities is easy to envision—as Jeanne Simpson demonstrates in "Slippery Sylvans Sliding Sleekly into the Writing Center—Or Preparing for Professional Competition" (1996). The scenario of professional competition for academic writing centers by such companies as Sylvan Learning Systems and Kaplan Education Centers is not a futuristic projection but is, instead, a current reality. For example, the September 19, 1997, issue of *The Chronicle of Higher Education* announces, "Tutoring Companies Take Over Remedial Teaching at Some Colleges" (Gose 1997). The article describes how "remedial education is becoming big business" as Kaplan and Sylvan are "designing, overseeing, and in some cases, actually teaching remedial courses at a handful of colleges" (A44). While the emphasis is on remedial education, it is easy to see how this approach could be extended to any aspect of writing instruction and thus could disintermediate writing centers and writing programs as well as traditional composition programs. Consider, for example, the case Ellen Earle Chaffee (1998) makes for "listening to the people we serve":

> When the public became increasingly dissatisfied with American automobiles, they turned to Japanese automobiles. A reasonably open market will eventually provide alternatives that respond to public frustration with the current products and services. Higher education is no exception. Accredited, for-profit postsecondary institutions like DeVry Institute, based in Chicago, are increasing in number and enrollment. Corporations spend more on in-house training than is spent on all of public and private higher education, and some are beginning to seek accreditation for their schools. Rapidly emerging technologies that bridge distances give such institutions huge potential markets at an affordable price with the added public benefit of convenience. (17)

Outsourcing will also influence the future of writing centers in the alliances higher education will create with business and industry. Disintermediation is often imposed on systems that have become obsolete, nonresponsive, or economically unfeasible. Alliances, however, are chosen and designed by the parties involved who seek mutual benefits in exchange for shared talents and resources. The history of higher education in America demonstrates undeniably that social trends shape the educational process, and it is crucial that writing-center professionals understand how current trends will redefine educational systems in the next century. To trace this argument is to see the history of the emergence of the writing center in academics and to speculate upon future trends. It is also to see that these social and political trends and the increasing financial difficulties within higher education point unmistakably to radical change: not only writing centers but even the academy itself is likely to be so altered that it will seem to have disappeared.

Like all societal constructs, writing centers are a product of their history, and that history is inseparable from the history of education in

America. O'Brien (1998) presents a conceptual history in which three epistemological stages have shaped the role of higher education in America. The first stage, from the colonial period to essentially the end of the nineteenth century, was a time in which "American higher education was dominantly religious and denominational. Colleges were the creatures of the various sects; the minister-president presided and decided in the light of the denominational dogma and decree" (xii). The second stage marked the rise of the research university in the twentieth century, which caused a "shift in authority away from the president to the faculty. In the old-style denominational colleges, the Truth was already known (at least the faithful so believed); one needed only to preach and practice the known. The research universities proclaimed that the truth is yet to be discovered" (xii). The third stage, which universities now occupy at the beginning of the twenty-first century, represents the deconstruction and redefinition of the purpose of the postmodern research university in terms of social relevance and service.

From O'Brien's description, it is easy to see the historical and ideological relationships the writing center has shared with the aims of higher education in America. Contrary to popular notions and to some of the writing-center literature itself, writing centers have a longer history in academics than many writers have allowed. The earliest published article appears in 1905 (Buck), and writing-center scholarship spans nearly a century of academic evolution and change. During this near century of growth, three modes of discourse about the writing center's role within the academy have predominated, and each reflects broader philosophical arguments conducted during the twentieth century about the function of education in society (Murphy 1991). Stanley Aronowitz and Henry A. Giroux (1985) define these three educational philosophies and sociopolitical currents as "the conservative, liberal, and radical debate over schooling" (iii). The conservative perspective envisions a schooling system in which "the mastery of techniques is equivalent to progress" (2); the liberal vision is of schooling as "a broad preparation for life, as an effective means to reproduce the type of society and individual consistent with western humanist traditions" (5); and the radical view is a politicized one in which the power struggles inherent in social systems also define educational processes. Thus, from the radical perspective, educators "are, perhaps unwittingly, clerks not only of the state, but also of the class that dominates it" (6). The purpose of education, thus, is to "promote ongoing forms of critique and a struggle against objective forces of oppression" (Giroux 1985, xviii).

This ideological history of writing centers mirrors O'Brien's philosophical history of American higher education. Clearly, for writing centers, the conservative view of education recodifies the early denominational emphasis upon known truths to be transmitted to a specific community of learners. Thus, "the model that underlies the conservative perspective is that of education as a type of regimented and highly authoritarian training for future roles within society" (Murphy 1991, 276). The writing centers established in the 1940s and 1950s exemplified the conservative approach by focusing primarily upon the remediation of weaker students in order to strengthen their writing skills and thus better prepare them for the academic experience (North 1984, 436). The primary emphasis was upon "task-oriented" students seeking the "markers" of an acceptable and uniform academic literacy (Murphy, 277). In this phase of their development, writing centers "remained closely tied to the scene of the classroom and became integral parts of the institutional desire to track students according to ability" (Boquet 1999, 467).

Undoubtedly, the emergence of the process movement in the 1970s and 1980s superseded the writing center's limited goals of imposing the contours of academic literacy upon remedial students and replaced those goals with a focus upon the learning styles and critical thinking skills of the individual student. This emphasis, in turn, gave rise to a concern for each student's voice and right of self-expression. But most of all the process movement became "a critique (or even outright rejection) of traditional, product-driven, rules-based, correctness-obsessed writing instruction" (Tobin 1994, 5). For writing centers emerging within the philosophical matrix of the process movement, this emphasis upon the writing and learning styles of the individual student represented a strident and revolutionary call to the ideals of the liberal philosophy of education and an equally strong rejection of the remedial goals imposed upon the writing center by the conservative creed of earlier decades. As Stephen M. North wrote in "The Idea of a Writing Center," a 1984 *College English* essay that is often considered the manifesto of the liberal or expressivist view of the writing center, "We are not here to serve, supplement, back up, complement, reinforce, or otherwise be defined by any external curriculum. We are here to talk to writers" (440).

While the conservative philosophy sought to strengthen the hegemony of traditional academic literacy and the liberal philosophy sought transformation of the individual student through "a spiritual sort of personal development—self-realization at whatever depth one understands the self" (Moffett 1994, 28), neither philosophy found a comfortable home in the writing center or provided a comfortable home for the writing center within the academy. The conservative philosophy tended to marginalize the writing center from the mainstream of academic instruction and into the peripheral concerns of remediation. The strongly critical and rebellious tone of the liberal philosophy, as expressed through the process movement, positioned writing centers as sites of nonconformity and nonidentification and produced a different type of marginalization from the central direction of academic policies and practices. In the liberal philosophy, writing-center practitioners were encouraged to view themselves as "renegades, outsiders, boundary dwellers, subversives" and to regard the writing center itself as the "writing outland" (Davis 1995, 7).

The irony of both movements is that—for all their philosophical and practical differences—neither movement paid much attention to "the larger cultural and social influences on individual authors" and continued to posit "the writer" in a way that erased "differences of race, class, gender, personality" (Tobin 1994, 8). Lisa Ede (1994) writes that most process theory did not acknowledge "the extent to which both its methods and its conclusions depended upon the reduction of students, in all their diversity, into a construct called the student writer, and of writing, with its rich multiplicity, into student writing" (35). It was, of course, a logical and historical progression that the writing center of the 1990s would turn its focus almost entirely to the social dimensions of the writer. By extension, it is equally logical that writing-center scholars would argue for the writing center as a site of social change. This "leftist or cultural critique" (Tobin, 6) of the writing center's role in the academy became an assertion of the writing center's right and social mission to challenge the central values of the academy. For example, in "Rearticulating the Work of the Writing Center," Nancy Maloney Grimm (1996) endorses the political agenda of opposition to "the hierarchical structure of higher education" (529) and a concomitant focus upon counterhegemony in both the structure and the purpose of writing-center practice:

> To rearticulate the work of the writing center in ways that avoid its implication in meritocratic myths about literacy, I will apply arguments about the nature of language and power from theorists such as Foucault, Gramsci, Vygotsky, Pratt, and Laclau and Mouffe to the writing center, a move that composition scholars who have aligned their work with a social justice mission will recognize. (525)

In a similar vein, by focusing on the "social justice mission" of the writing center, Marilyn M. Cooper (1994) and Cynthia Haynes-Burton (1994) have argued that writing centers are politically charged sites whose primary role is to challenge the power, value, and purpose of dominant discourses within the academy.

We believe the "social justice mission" that the cultural studies agenda created for writing centers has been the most instrumental force in redefining the writing center's complex and conflicted relationship to the academy. We hold this belief for two reasons: first, the social justice mission extensively engaged the writing center in critiquing the values of society at large and thus "opened the doors" of the writing center to interaction with other social institutions and forums. Second, the social justice mission and the cultural studies agenda often drew upon language philosophers to argue for an assessment of academic literacy in the light of other prevailing discourses in society. As James Moffett (1994) states, "It was also only when we looked beyond academic walls that we began to open up the range of discourse that students might write in" (23). As a result, Moffett claims, "Learning sites and opportunities will then be located all over a community and include apprenticeships, tutoring, and other arrangements [that] will change drastically not how we think today about learning to write but how we may organize for it" (27).

The issue of how to organize for writing instruction in the twenty-first century is the most crucial one the academy and the writing center will face. In 1982—in an essay appropriately titled "Winds of Change: Thomas Kuhn and the Revolution in the Teaching of Writing"—Maxine Hairston proclaimed that the shift in writing pedagogy from a product-centered to a process-centered theory indicated that the profession was "probably in the first stages of a [Kuhnian] paradigm shift" (77). We contend that the twenty-first century will represent for writing centers and for the academy a "revolution in the teaching of writing" that will be many times more significant and powerful than the Kuhnian conceptual paradigm shift Hairston described. Indeed, the shift many social theorists envision involves the dismantling of traditional academic structures and the creation of the nontraditional "academic conglomerate" (O'Brien 1998, 20) with multiple identities, roles, and purposes within business, technology, and industry. Slaughter and Leslie (1997) call this new, nontraditional "academic conglomerate" the "entrepreneurial university," and Tierney (1998) calls it the "responsive university." All these writers have in common the belief that the university of the twenty-first century will have social relationships and partnerships as its core principle of action and identity.

Re-creating the academy also means reorienting the goals of academic life and structures. Clark Kerr (1994) argues that, within this socially responsive model for academic life, faculty members will have to be less committed to the academic community as an isolated enclave and more committed to economic factors, including funding agencies and outside employers. Slaughter and Leslie (1997) contend that "as departments and centers are reconfigured to match market opportunities, academics may find their corporate and government counterparts a more meaningful reference group than their professions or academic disciplines" (227).

For writing centers, this reconfiguring of identities will represent burgeoning growth and the most dramatic shift in roles and functions in the hundred-year history of writing centers. While the struggle for legitimacy within the academy defined the writing center's first one hundred years, the next century will find writing centers forming social alliances and finding new identities within technology and industry. This refocusing will occur as the result of extensive social changes that are also redefining American higher education. O'Brien (1998) reminds his readers that the university has not always been understood in its current sense and warns that the institution itself may change radically with economic restructuring. "If the historical entity 'university' is to have a future," he cautions, "it will need to examine its *institutional* assumptions" (4–5, emphasis in original). Historically, the "*institutional* assumptions" that surround writing centers have been that writing centers are tutorial sites located within the academy. While writing-center theorists may argue about the best location for the writing center—from freestanding units to sites within the English department or writing-across-the-curriculum (WAC) program—the arguments have always focused on intra-academy sites, roles, and organizational structures. The discussions, too, have remained largely philosophical or conceptual—a position that we view as politically naïve. By way of example, let us return to Maxine Hairston's 1982 claim that the shift from product to process was a paradigm shift on the level of a Kuhnian revolution in science. Rooted in the belief that changes in institutional practices and goals are largely driven by philosophical changes, Hairston's argument fails to account for social changes occurring at the time of the process movement's ascendance in the academy. Open admission policies in the 1960s and 1970s and changes in the academic population as a result had a far greater effect in determining a new pedagogy focused on individual learning and writing styles than did the replacement of one paradigm by another.

We would argue that this same level of political naïveté continues to inform much of the scholarship on writing centers. While the cultural-studies movement has been successful in focusing upon the cultural and political contexts that surround and shape individual writers, it has been far less successful in getting the writing-center community to look at the social and political realities that will determine that community's future. Some writing-center theorists do emphasize the impact of political contexts and struggles within the academy, but few discuss the political realities of social changes external to the academy yet essential to its functioning. We contend that the most pressing of these social forces are funding for higher education and demographic changes in the populations that support the educational system. While conservative, liberal, and radical writing-center theorists might prefer to focus on the "moralizing mission" of education in the improvement and empowerment of individual writers, O'Brien (1998) claims that a different emphasis is at work in the political dynamics of the academy: "Moral arguments about the nature of higher education might be regarded as an interesting diversion, but there is a more pressing issue for contemporary higher education: not morals, but money" (xv). He goes on to argue that in the twenty-first century funding for higher education will decline significantly, noting that funders are already demanding that "higher education be more 'productive,' more efficient, and more effective." The limits that will result from budgetary restrictions are "as likely to be political as philosophical, market driven as moral. . . . When the coffers close, who will decide on the intellectual survivors?" (xv–xvi). And he concludes his argument in this fashion:

> Practical first: universities in the United States (and worldwide) are under enormous financial pressures. It is clear that the percentage of national income expended on the growth of higher education during the roughly twenty years from 1960 to 1980 will not be expanded or even sustained. Financial crisis raises institutional issues. Will there be a Department of Greek? Can one afford high-level specialties? Can one afford liberal arts? The financial constraints of higher education may suggest not only minor trimming but also total institutional restructuring. (4)

The "total institutional restructuring" writing centers will face in the twenty-first century will undoubtedly involve moving away from traditional and classical concepts of the academy—however cherished those concepts may be—toward the politics and policies of the entrepreneurial university. The reason for this change is dramatically simple: the traditional academy itself is disappearing and being transformed by "academic capitalism" and entrepreneurship into a complex of partnerships between academics and industry.

To illustrate a few of the partnerships that are already being made—partnerships that ought to be particularly instructive to writing-center professionals—we turn to some of the recent activities of Sylvan Learning Systems, Inc., a twenty-year-old company that began as a chain of tutoring centers serving students in elementary and high schools. Since Douglas L. Becker and a partner purchased the company in 1991, it has expanded its operations in a number of areas.

These activities read like a textbook illustration of the "digital economy" described by Tapscott (1996). Forming specialized, limited alliances with various companies, Sylvan has developed programs that fit educational niches at all levels, including the most advanced. For instance, Caliber Learning Network, a partnership between Sylvan and MCI, has piloted a distance-education project with the School of Medicine and School of Continuing Education at Johns Hopkins University. In this venture, Caliber provided not only technical assistance but also some of the funding (Blumenstyk 1997, A23), a clear reminder that the private, for-profit sector is an important resource for schools chronically in need. More recently, in January 1999, it was announced that Sylvan would start a network of for-profit universities in Europe. This network would not create new schools but work with existing programs, building up those that are already successful and improving others. The project will be headed by Joseph D. Duffey, who will leave his position as Director of the U. S. Information Agency to assume the post. Previously Duffey had served as president of American University and as chancellor of the University of Massachusetts at Amherst (Lively and Blumenstyk 1999, A43).

The participation of such a distinguished educator as Duffey and such a prestigious institution as Johns Hopkins is an unmistakable indication of the current climate in education. That climate is even more clearly defined in a letter to *The Chronicle of Higher Education*. Writing in response to the report of the remedial programs being developed by Sylvan and Kaplan (see Gose 1997), George L. Findlen (1997) challenged some of the assumptions he found underlying that report:

> Implying that for-profit service providers cannot teach or train misses the point. The variability of learners will always outstrip the ability of some teachers to produce the results that society needs. It is time to let companies like Kaplan Learning Services and Sylvan Learning Systems have a chance. It is results that society needs, not job protection for those who may not be able to get those results. (B10)

Findlen's concluding call for results echoes a frustration with education often expressed in today's public forums, whether on the floors of state legislatures or on radio talk shows. Yet Findlen is speaking from a vantage point from within the academy, and, as Dean of General Education and Educational Services at Western Wisconsin Technical College, he presumably has a direct impact on how educational services will be delivered to students there—services likely to include a writing center.

Though attitudes like Findlen's may be seen as a challenge to the status quo, we see the writing center as uniquely positioned to embrace these changes and to prosper within them. The collaborative learning environment of the writing center is highly "portable" and can be easily resituated within business and industry. For example, writing centers currently teach writing and critical thinking skills to students who take positions in business and industry in which they are "retrained" in these same skills by the corporations that employ them. This duplication of effort and of resources is especially problematic when, as Chaffee (1998) points out, "corporations spend more on in-house training than is spent on all of public and private higher education" (17). Disintermediation may remove the academic writing center as the expendable "middle man" in this scenario; however, the wiser course of action is for writing-center professionals to seek the types of alliances with corporations that would enable writing-center professionals to shape and to participate in the "in-house training" that corporations provide. This scenario is both feasible and economical. An even more likely scenario, though, is that writing-center professionals and the writing center itself will sever ties with the academy and move into corporate settings as the primary provider of in-house training in writing and critical thinking skills.

Academicians undoubtedly will struggle with assuming new identities as participants in the corporate structure of business and industry, but "relative isolation from the market" is an unlikely option for academicians in the future economy, which will value faculty-applied research and skills in postindustrial corporate settings (Slaughter and Leslie 1997, 7). While reconceptualizing both roles and identities may be a difficult process for most writing-center professionals who have come to the writing center through traditional academic routes, the alternative is not an option. If academic writing centers are disintermediated by funding priorities and by reduced options for the growth and expansion of higher education in America, then the writing center—and the academy itself—may well disappear from the public sector.

Works Cited

Aronowitz, S., and H. Giroux. 1985. *Education Under Siege*. South Hadley, MA: Bergin and Garvey.

Benjamin, R., and S. Carroll. 1998. "The Implications of the Changed Environment for Governance in Higher Education." In *The Responsive University: Restructuring for High Performance*, edited by W. G. Tierney, 92–119. Baltimore: Johns Hopkins University Press.

Blumenstyk, G. 1997. "Elite Private Universities Get Serious About Distance Learning." *The Chronicle of Higher Education*, 20 June, A23.

Boquet, E. H. 1999. "'Our Little Secret': A History of Writing Centers, Pre- to Post-Open Admissions." *College Composition and Communication* 50 (3): 463–82.

Braskamp, L., and J. F. Wergin. 1998. "Forming New Social Partnerships." In *The Responsive University: Restructuring for High Performance*, edited by W. G. Tierney, 62–91. Baltimore: Johns Hopkins University Press.

Buck, P. M. Jr. 1905. "Laboratory Method in English Composition." *National Education Association Journal of Proceedings and Addresses of the 43rd Annual Meeting. St. Louis, 27 June–1 July 1904*. Winona, MN: National Education Association.

Chaffee, E. E. 1998. "Listening to the People We Serve." In *The Responsive University: Restructuring for High Performance*, edited by W. G. Tierney, 13–37. Baltimore: Johns Hopkins University Press.

Cooper, M. M. 1994. "Really Useful Knowledge: A Cultural Studies Agenda for Writing Centers." *The Writing Center Journal* 14 (2): 97–111.

Davis, K. 1995. "Life Outside the Boundary: History and Direction in the Writing Center." *Writing Lab Newsletter* 20 (2): 5–7.

Ede, L. 1994. "Reading the Writing Process." In *Taking Stock: The Writing Process Movement in the 90s*, edited by L. Tobin and T. Newkirk, 31–43. Portsmouth, NH: Boynton/Cook.

Findlen, G. L. 1997. Letter to the editor. *The Chronicle of Higher Education*, 24 October, B10.

Giroux, H. A. 1985. Introduction to *The Politics of Education: Culture, Power, and Liberation*, by Paulo Freire, xi–xxv. South Hadley, MA: Bergin and Garvey.

Gose, B. 1997. "Tutoring Companies Take Over Remedial Teaching at Some Colleges." *The Chronicle of Higher Education*, 19 September, A44–A45.

Grimm, N. M. 1996. "Rearticulating the Work of the Writing Center." *College Composition and Communication* 47 (4): 523–48.

Hairston, M. 1982. "The Winds of Change: Thomas Kuhn and the Revolution in the Teaching of Writing." *College Composition and Communication* 33 (1): 76–88.

Haynes-Burton, C. 1994. "'Hanging Your Alias on Their Scene': Writing Centers, Graffiti, and Style." *The Writing Center Journal* 14 (2): 112–24.

Kerr, C. 1994. "Knowledge, Ethics, and the New Academic Culture." *Change* 26 (1): 8–15.

Lively, K., and G. Blumenstyk. 1999. "Sylvan Learning Systems to Start a Network of For-Profit Universities Overseas." *The Chronicle of Higher Education*, 29 January, A43.

Moffett, J. 1994. "Reading the Writing Process Movement: Coming Out Right." In *Taking Stock: The Writing Process Movement in the 90s*, edited by L. Tobin and T. Newkirk, 17–30. Portsmouth, NH: Boynton/Cook.

Murphy, C. 1991. "Writing Centers in Context: Responding to Current Educational Theory." In *The Writing Center: New Directions*, edited by R. Wallace and J. Simpson, 276–88. New York: Garland.

North, S. 1984. "The Idea of a Writing Center." *College English* 46 (5): 433–46.

O'Brien, G. D. 1998. *All the Essential Half-Truths About Higher Education.* Chicago: Chicago University Press.

Simpson, J. 1996. "Slippery Sylvans Sliding Sleekly into the Writing Center— Or Preparing for Professional Competition." *Writing Lab Newsletter* 21 (1): 1–4.

Slaughter, S., and L. L. Leslie. 1997. *Academic Capitalism: Politics, Policies, and the Entrepreneurial University.* Baltimore: Johns Hopkins University Press.

Tapscott, D. 1996. *The Digital Economy: Promise and Peril in the Age of Networked Intelligence.* New York: McGraw-Hill.

Tierney, W. G. 1998. "On the Road to Recovery and Renewal: Reinventing Academe." In *The Responsive University: Restructuring for High Performance*, edited by W. G. Tierney, 92–119. Baltimore: Johns Hopkins University Press.

Tobin, L. 1994. "How the Writing Process Was Born—and Other Conversion Narratives." In *Taking Stock: The Writing Process Movement in the 90s*, edited by L. Tobin and T. Newkirk, 1–14. Portsmouth, NH: Boynton/Cook.

Contributors

Deborah H. Burns is Associate Professor of English and former Director of the Writing Center at Merrimack College. She has published articles on writing-center theory and practice and has developed the Writing Fellows Program, in which advanced undergraduates employ a social-rhetorical approach to discipline-specific tutoring. She is a member of the Intercollegiate Electronic Democracy Project and has developed many distance education courses using Web-based technology.

Peter Carino is Professor of English and Director of the Writing Center at Indiana State University, where he teaches American literature and technical writing. He has authored two basic writing textbooks and has published several essays on writing centers, composition pedagogy, American literature, and baseball literature. Two of his essays on writing centers won consecutive National Writing Centers Association awards for Best Article in 1995 and 1996. He is a past president of the East Central Writing Centers Association and served seven years on the ECWCA Executive Board.

Pamela B. Childers, Caldwell Chair of Composition at The McCallie School, directs the WAC-based writing center and teaches an interdisciplinary science course. Treasurer of the Assembly on Computers in English and former NWCA President, Pam gives writing workshops and presentations to secondary and college teachers internationally. She writes a column for *academic writing*. Her books include *The High School Writing Center: Establishing and Maintaining One* (NCTE, 1989; NWCA Outstanding Scholarship Award), *Programs and Practices: Writing Across the Secondary School Curriculum* (Boynton/Cook, 1994) with Anne Ruggles Gere and Art Young, and *ARTiculating: Teaching Writing in a Visual World* (Boynton/Cook, 1998) with Eric Hobson and Joan Mullin.

Jane Cogie is Associate Professor of English and Director of the Writing Center at Southern Illinois University at Carbondale. Her articles on writing center issues have appeared in *The Writing Center Journal* and *WPA: Writing Program Administration*. Her current research interests include the politics of writing-center administration and the intersection of pedagogy and ethics in tutoring dialect and English-as-a-second-language speakers.

Richard Colby is a writing-center consultant and composition instructor at California State University, San Bernardino. He is presently researching the impact of technology on writing and other literacy acts.

Kathy Evertz has directed the University Studies First-Year Program at the University of Wyoming since 1997. Before assuming her current position, she taught for eight years in the Department of English at UW. She directed the Wyoming Conference on English from 1993 to 1997. At UW she has worked with faculty in writing-across-the-curriculum projects. She has authored articles and given conference presentations on the relationship between writing centers and writing across the curriculum. In addition to teaching composition at UW, she has taught courses in art history in the Honors Program, American Studies, and Art. She has researched and given presentations on the life and art of Virginia Frederick Large, a Saratoga, Wyoming, artist.

Katherine M. Fischer, M.F.A., directs the Writing Lab and teaches classes in writing and literature at Clarke College in Dubuque, Iowa. Her academic articles and chapters focus on writing-center practice; technology-enriched instruction; and teaching creative writing, composition, and literature. Her poetry, nonfiction, and fiction appear frequently in magazines, journals, and literary presses. In her writing, she struggles to see the connections between the world as it is written and the world as it reveals itself in nature.

Carmen M. Fye is currently teaching English composition as an associate faculty member at Mount San Jacinto College and California State University, San Bernardino. Research interests include computers and writing theory with an emphasis in feminist and composition theory.

Muriel Harris, Professor of English, founded and continues to direct the Purdue University Writing Lab, and founded and continues to serves as editor of the *Writing Lab Newsletter*. She has authored *The Prentice Hall Reference Guide to Grammar and Usage* (fourth edition, 1999), *The Writer's FAQs: A Pocket Handbook* (Prentice-Hall, 2000), and *Teaching One-to-One: The Writing Conference* (NCTE, 1986), plus numerous book chapters, articles, and conference presentations, all of which focus on writing center theory, pedagogy, practice, and OWLs. Her preference for the term *lab* (as discussed in this book) is evident in having named the *Writing Lab Newsletter* and Purdue's OWL (online writing lab). Harris was the recipient of the 2000 Conference on College Composition and Communication Exemplar Award.

Carol Peterson Haviland is Associate Professor of English and Writing Center Director at California State University, San Bernardino. She teaches graduate and undergraduate courses in rhetoric and composition, and her scholarly interests include writing centers, writing across the curriculum, feminist theories, collaboration, and intellectual property. She has a number of articles and book chapters, the book *Weaving Knowledge Together* (NWCA Press, 1998), and is coauthoring a new book, *Teaching Writing in the Late Age of Print*. She also serves on the National Writing Centers Association board.

Eric Hobson is Associate Professor of Humanities at the Albany College of Pharmacy, where he directs the school's faculty-development efforts. The 1998 president of the National Writing Centers Association, Eric is a national leader in developing writing centers and writing-across-the-curriculum programs in health-care education. His books include *ARTiculating: Teaching Writing in a Visual World* (Boynton/Cook, 1998) with Pamela Childers and Joan Mullin, *Writing Center Perspectives* (NWCA, 1995) with Christina Murphy and Byron Stay, and *Reading and Writing in High Schools* (NEA, 1990) with R. Baird Schuman. He edited *Wiring the Writing Center* (Utah State University Press, 1998), winner of the 1999 National Writing Center Association Outstanding Scholarship Award.

Joe Law is Associate Professor of English and Coordinator of Writing Across the Curriculum at Wright State University in Dayton, Ohio. His publications include *Writing Centers: An Annotated Bibliography* (Greenwood, 1996) with Christina Murphy and Steve Sherwood, and *Landmark Essays on Writing Centers* (Hermagoras, 1995) with Christina Murphy, winners of the Outstanding Scholarship award from the National Writing Centers Association for the best book of the year in 1997 and 1996, respectively. *The Theory and Criticism of Virtual Texts: An Annotated Bibliography*, which he coedited with Lory Hawkes and Christina Murphy, was published in 2000 (Greenwood).

Carrie Shively Leverenz is Associate Professor of English and Director of Composition at Texas Christian University. She teaches undergraduate and graduate courses on writing and rhetoric and is currently working on a book, *Doing the Right Thing: Ethical Issues in Institutionalized Writing Instruction*. At the time of the study described in this collection, she was the Director of the Reading/Writing Center and Computer-Supported Writing Classrooms at Florida State University.

Kelly Lowe is Associate Professor of English and Director of Writing Programs at Mount Union College in Alliance, Ohio. He has published pieces in the *Writing Lab Newsletter* and *Reforming College Composition: Writing the Wrongs*. He is also editor of the National Writing Centers Association newsletter. He is working on a book about sport and metaphor.

Barry M. Maid is Professor of Technical Communication at Arizona State University East, where he is at work on developing a new program in Multimedia Writing and Technical Communication. Previously, he was Professor of Rhetoric and Writing at the University of Arkansas at Little Rock, where he served as Director of the Writing Center, Director of First Year Composition, and Chair of the Department of English. His present interests combine many of the past hats he has worn. He tries to combine his administrative experience, his interest in technology (both computers and video), his professional interest in technical communication, and his work with personality theory.

Margaret J. Marshall is Associate Professor and Director of Composition at the University of Miami. Previously, she was the Director of the University of Pittsburgh's Writing Center. Marshall earned her Ph.D. from the Joint Program in English and Education at the University of Michigan in 1991 and spent a year as a member of the University of Michigan's English Composition Board. Her book *Contesting Cultural Rhetorics: Public Discourse and Education, 1890-1900* (University of Michigan Press, 1995) examines conceptions of education in popular magazines. A book on the rhetoric of professionalizing teaching is forthcoming from the Studies in Writing and Rhetoric series published by Southern Illinois University Press.

Pat McQueeney is Assistant Professor of English at Johnson County Community College in Overland Park, Kansas, where she teaches freshman–sophomore composition. From 1986–1999, she was affiliated with Writing Consulting (formerly the Writing Center) at the University of Kansas. She was the writing-across-the-curriculum specialist in the office and Director of Writing Consulting from 1998–1999, which included a WAC service for faculty and a writing center for students. Her Ph.D. is in composition theory from the University of Kansas (1995). Current research interests include WAC, academic discourse, and professional writing. She is coauthoring a WAC-based composition textbook designed for community college and liberal arts college writers.

Christina Murphy is Associate Dean of the College of Humanities and Social Sciences and Professor of English at The William Paterson University of New Jersey. Murphy has served as the president of the National Writing Centers Association and as the editor of *Composition Studies*. Her coedited publications include *The Theory and Criticism of Virtual Texts: An Annotated Bibliography, 1988–1999* (Greenwood, 2001); *Writing Centers: An Annotated Bibliography* (Greenwood, 1996); *Landmark Essays on Writing Centers* (Hermagoras/Erlbaum, 1995); *The St. Martin's Sourcebook for Writing Tutors* (St. Martin's, 1995); and *Writing Center Perspectives* (NWCA, 1995).

Jane Nelson has directed the Writing Center at the University of Wyoming since 1991. Prior to returning to the University of Wyoming in 1982, she taught for five years at Texas A&M University. She has worked with faculty in a variety of disciplines on classroom research projects dealing with student writing, and she has coauthored numerous articles on such subjects as computers and writing, writing-center theory and practice, and writing in specific disciplines. She has also published several articles on Western American writers and is currently working on a biography of an early settler in the North Platte Valley near Saratoga, Wyoming. She is a past president of the Rocky Mountain Writing Centers Association.

Linda K. Shamoon is Professor of English, Director of the College Writing Program, and Director of the Faculty Institute on Writing at the University of Rhode Island. She has published articles on the research paper, writing across the curriculum, the place of rhetoric in composition programs, and writing-center practices. She is coeditor, with Rebecca Moore Howard and Sandra Jameison, of *Coming of Age: The Advanced Writing Curriculum* (Boynton/Cook, 2000). She is a founding member of the Intercollegiate Electronic Democracy Project. In addition to directing the writing program, she also serves as a regional consultant for writing across the curriculum.

Jeanne H. Simpson, who has recently retired, was a professor of English and Assistant Vice President for Academic Affairs at Eastern Illinois University. She earned her B.A. from Texas Tech University, her M.A. from the University of Texas at Austin, and her Doctor of Arts degree in rhetoric and composition from Illinois State University. She established Eastern's writing center in 1981 and directed it for nine years. She was a founding member of the National Writing Centers Association and served as its third president. With Ray Wallace, she coedited *The Writing Center: New Directions* (Garland, 1991).

John Trimbur is Professor of Writing and Rhetoric and Director of the Technical, Scientific, and Professional Communication program at Worcester Polytechnic Institute. Recent publications include the textbooks *The Call to Write* (Longman, 1999) and, with Diana George, *Reading Culture* (Longman, 2000, fourth ed.) and the edited collection *Popular Literacy: Studies in Cultural Practices and Poetics* (University of Pittsburgh Press, 2001).

James K. Upton teaches at Burlington Community High School in Burlington, Iowa. He holds a B.A. and an M.A. from Western Illinois University. He has been a facilitator in the Iowa Writing Project for more than a decade. Upton has researched and developed The Write Place, an NCTE Center of Excellence award–winning center. He places great emphasis on a center without walls, and pushing the envelope to expand writing and learning skills across the curriculum. He has chaired the "mindbody" faculty team for the past five years, working on utilizing brain research in helping students with the writing and learning process.